SPEAKEASY

SPEAKEASY

200 UNDERGROUND COCKTAILS

BENNY ROFF

Illustrated by Georgia Perry

hardie grant books

This book is dedicated to Leilani Ravalico,
who is shaping up to be a lovely drinking companion,
and to anyone who's managed to have a good time
despite the best intentions of legislators.

CONTENTS

Introduction

'Prohibition is better than no liquor at all.'

Will Rogers
Circus Cowboy, Movie Star and Social Commentator

The Speakeasy was the great social crucible of its day.
Mobsters, who rocketed to wealth and power on the back
of prohibition, could mingle with movie stars, alcoholic
writers and the wealthy establishment. Speakeasies were too
expensive to be truly inclusive, but if one could foot the mark-
up on booze, then social pedigree would prove no impediment
to having a good time. Speakeasies were also open to women
in a way that saloons had never previously been. Having just
won the right to vote, women also achieved new freedoms in
their social lives, courtships and sexuality – all washed down
with a dry martini.

Glossary of 1920s slang

APPLESAUCE an expression of incredulity

BANK'S CLOSED no kissing!

BEE'S KNEES very good

BERRIES very good

BIMBO a tough guy

CAKE-EATER a ladies man

CASH OR CHEQUE? do we kiss now or later?

DADDY a boyfriend or male lover, particularly one who foots the bills

FOUR FLUSHER a bluffer, not necessarily a good one

GIGGLE WATER booze

HALF-SEAS OVER smashfaced drunk

HARD BOILED a tough guy

HAYBURNER a gas-guzzling car

HIGH-HAT a supercilious rebuff

HIT ON ALL SIXES performs 100% (as in 'all six cylinders' or 'fire in the engine')

HOOFER dancer

HORSEFEATHERS same as applesauce

HOTSY-TOTSY good looking

JAKE fine, as in 'everything's Jake'

KISSER mouth

LET'S BLOUSE let's leave

LIVE WIRE the life of the party

MAZUMA money

ON A TOOT on a bender

ON THE LAM on the run from the law

PETTING PANTRY a cinema, as in somewhere to make out

RITZY fancy, expensive, like the Ritz Hotel

SAYS YOU yet another expression of incredulity

SCOFFLAW one who scoffs at the law, a drinker despite prohibition

SHEBA a sexually attractive woman

SHEIK a sexually attractive man

SLUMMING mixing with people of a lower social class for entertainment

SNORKY well dressed. Al Capone's close friends called him 'Snorky'

SPIFFLICATED same as half-seas over

SULTAN OF SWAT a nickname for Babe Ruth

SWELL very good

THE CAT'S PAJAMAS the best

TIGHT drunk

WET a political movement against prohibition. A member of that movement.

Notes on some ingredients

Vermouth & Quinquina

Vermouth in the 1920s came
in two basic varieties:

RED VERMOUTH or SWEET VERMOUTH
(often called Italian vermouth in the old days)
is quite sweet and is made by the French
and Italians. A special mention should be
made of Cocchi Vermouth di Torino, which
is called for in several recipes. It has a
totally different flavour profile to regular
red vermouth and shouldn't be substituted.
You can find it online if nowhere else.

DRY VERMOUTH was very important in
the 1920s, but has fallen from grace a
little. The most famous French vermouth
come from Noilly Prat and Dolin.

QUINQUINA are wine-based aperitifs like
vermouth, but they also contain cinchona
bark, which is the main ingredient in tonic
water. It staves off malaria and has a bitter
flavour. If you look hard you can find Dubonnet
and Byrrh, which were both popular in the
1920s. What you can't find is Kina Lillet, as
its production ceased in the 1980s. There
are two substitutes that are commonly used,
though they may be hard to find: Kina l'Aero
d'Or is made by Tempus Fugit Spirits and is
a modern attempt to recreate Kina Lillet, and
Cocchi Americano is an Italian quinquina
that has a similar flavour. The internet can
be your friend when purchasing any of these
products and it is totally worth the effort!

Liqueurs

Liqueurs can be a tricky one; the French make a lot of good ones. Special mention must be made of a few liqueurs, as they were very popular in the 1920s but are a little more obscure now. They also can be found through the magic of the internet, thanks in no small part to the craft cocktail movement.

The most important liqueurs in the 1920s seem to have been:

CURAÇAO or TRIPLE SEC are both sweet liqueurs made from bitter oranges. If your curaçao is blue, please don't use it in these drinks.

MARASCHINO has nothing to do with the day-glow cherries that go by the same name.

The best-known brand is Luxardo, which I have mentioned by name in an attempt to keep the sickly cherry juice out of the drinks.

SWEDISH PUNSCH, also known as arrack punch or caloric punch, is Sweden's national liqueur. It is made from an Indonesian spirit distilled from red rice and sugar cane juice. The most common brand is Carlshamn's Flaggpunsch.

CRÈME DE NOYAUX is made from apricot pits, much like amaretto, which is a good substitute. Unfortunately there is at least one brand from North America that uses almond flavouring and isn't the real deal. Tempus Fugit Spirits have recreated a good one, otherwise use an Italian amaretto.

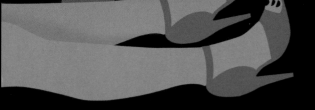

Absinthe

All the recipes in this book that call for absinthe want the French style, which are heavily anise flavoured. Please don't try to substitute the Bohemian style, which is more bitter and less aromatic. You could probably get away with using pastis (like Pernod or Ricard) for most of the recipes.

Gin

Far and away the most popular spirit of the day, the 1920s saw the tail end of some styles that were popular in the nineteenth century.

DRY GIN or *LONDON DRY GIN* is the predominant style of gin today, which has a punchy juniper flavour.

PLYMOUTH GIN has a milder flavour than dry gin. The branded Plymouth gin is the only official style, but there are modern gins with subtle flavours and citrus forwards that substitute. You could also try using a Dutch Jonge Jenever that is also mild with juniper and has a much less rye malt flavour than other Dutch gins.

OLD TOM GIN was very popular in the nineteenth and early twentieth centuries. It is spicier than Plymouth gin and is notable for its relatively high sugar content.

YELLOW GIN has spent time in oak barrels. Many years ago, gin wasn't bottled, but like most liquids was transported in oak barrels. This tradition of lightly ageing gin has persisted intermittently and these days there are several brands on the market. You can substitute London Dry for yellow gin in these recipes, but not the other way around.

Rum

There are two basic varieties of rum called for in this book:

WHITE RUM is usually aged and filtered to make a clear product. It is far lighter tasting than dark rum, though some are aged up to six years before filtration and become quite complex.

DARK RUM by which I mean a properly aged rum with a syrupy quality. Go for something at least seven years old.

Bitters

While there is a dizzying array of bitters available these days, in the 1920s there were three main varieties in use: Angostura bitters, Peychaud's bitters and orange bitters. The first two are brand names and there are many types of orange bitters available, which are a valuable addition to any bar. The other type of bitters included in the recipes is Boker's bitters, which was very popular in the nineteenth century and went out of business when prohibition came in. There is at least one modern attempt to copy it, available as Boker's bitters.

Some Cocktail Equipment

Cocktail shakers

The two most common types of cocktail shaker we see today are the Boston shaker and the cobbler shaker. The Boston shaker is the type one sees in cocktail bars with a metal cup and a matching glass that is stuck in the top to seal it before shaking. This type of shaker requires a separate strainer to stop the big pieces of ice from going into the drink or a finer strainer to fine-strain a drink. The cobbler shaker is the type one sees in people's homes: it has a metal cup, a metal lid with a built in strainer and a metal cap to cover during shaking. They often become impossible to open once used, so they aren't favoured by most bartenders.

Mixing glass

This is any type of glass with a large enough volume to stir ice around in. The most common type in bars is a thick tapered glass with a 480 ml (1 US pint) volume that comes as part of a Boston shaker. It is commonly paired with a bar spoon, which is a long-handled spoon with a twisted metal handle to facilitate rotating it in the palm of your hands. It is okay to use any other type of spoon or even chopsticks to mix. If no spoon is available, you can get a pretty good result by gently moving the glass in circles so that the contents are moving around. Just be careful not to actually shake the drink and incorporate air into it; a stirred drink must be mixed very gently so as to remain crystal clear and not over dilute.

Strainers

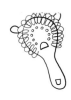

The Boston shaker is often paired with a hawthorne strainer, which is a round affair with a handle and a spring around the outside to press into the rim of the shaker. It will stop large pieces of ice and fruit from leaving the shaker, but won't strain out smaller pieces of ice etc. so it is often used in combination with a fine-strainer, which is any strainer with a very fine mesh. I use a double-meshed stainless steel strainer in my bar, but a tea strainer will do a pretty good job and will be very easy to find. For practicality, it is useful to use a small strainer that will fit into a cocktail glass without knocking it over. A julep strainer is sometimes used instead of a hawthorne – it is a large, round perforated spoon with a short handle that looks very cool, which to my mind is its greatest advantage.

Glassware

Cocktail glass

Often called a Martini glass, a cocktail glass is used to serve drinks up or straight up – that is to say 'without ice'. For the purposes of this book, feel free to use a champagne coupe wherever a cocktail glass is called for or vice versa.

Old-fashioned

Sometimes called a rocks glass, the old-fashioned is a short glass that is used to serve cocktails on the rocks (or simply rocks). They come in various sizes with very large ones being designated a double old-fashioned.

Highball

This tall, wide glass is used for serving fizzy mixed drinks such as highballs (duh!). It holds a similar volume of liquid to the collins glass, so feel free to switch them around for convenience.

Champagne flute

A narrow-sided, tapered, stemmed glass that is excellent for preserving Champagne's effervescence and bouquet.

Wine goblet

A wine glass with a squat, round, tapered bowl. You can use a small wine glass instead.

Champagne coupe

The Champagne coupe is sometimes called a Marie Antoinette after the erroneous supposition that it was modelled on her breast, or indeed the breast of several other famous ladies of her era. The glass predates them all, and is a terrible thing from which to drink Champagne. It does, however, make a lovely cocktail glass and makes you feel rather glamorous, especially in evening wear.

Collins glass

Taller and narrower than a highball, the collins glass has straight sides. It is the glass of choice for a Tom Collins, or several other refreshing concoctions, but a highball will often do in a pinch.

Julep cup

This is the traditional vessel in which to make and serve a mint julep or its variants. It is a tapered cup made of sterling silver that achieves the right frostiness when the drink is mixed properly. Juleps also taste lovely in glass!

Syrup & Cordial Recipes

Grenadine

Grenadine is a pomegranate cordial that unfortunately is rarely made from pomegranates. Please don't use cheap grenadine in these recipes, only because it tastes terrible. There are some good brands out there, but it is very easy to make your own. You can use unsweetened pomegranate juice or you can juice your own.

Cut open a pomegranate, scrape all the seeds into a food mill with a medium plate and turn it until all the juice is extracted. If you juice your own, you can put the seeds back into the juice after you've measured it and heat them with the juice and sugar, then strain them out after it's cooled (it adds a slight nuttiness to the finished product). Citric acid will increase the shelf life, but isn't really necessary if you refrigerate it.

250 ml (8½ fl oz) pomegranate juice
250 g (9 oz) sugar
½ teaspoon citric acid (optional)

Put all the ingredients into a saucepan and mix very well. Bring slowly to a simmer and stir until the sugar is dissolved. Remove from the heat immediately and cool before use.

Sugar syrup

500 g (1 lb 2 oz) sugar
250 ml (8½ fl oz) water

METHOD 1 – high-speed blender
Put the ingredients in a high-speed blender and blend on high until the sugar is completely dissolved (about 1 minute).

METHOD 2 – blender
Bring the water to the boil then pour it into a blender with the sugar. Blend until the sugar is completely dissolved (about 1 minute).

METHOD 3 – microwave
Put the ingredients into a microwave-proof container and stir well. Cook on high for 3–5 minutes. Remove and stir. If the sugar is not completely dissolved, repeat until it is.

METHOD 4 – stovetop
Put the ingredients into a saucepan, stir well and bring to the boil. When the sugar is completely dissolved, remove from the heat. Allow to cool a little and fine-strain.

Clove syrup

250 g (9 oz) sugar
500 ml (17 fl oz) water
12 g (½ oz) whole cloves

Put all the ingredients into a saucepan, stir well and bring to the boil, simmering until the mixture is reduced by half. Remove from the heat, allow to cool a little and strain through a coffee filter.

Ginger syrup

20 g (¾ oz) fresh ginger, peeled
  and thinly sliced
250 g (9 oz) caster (superfine) sugar
250 ml (8½ fl oz) water

Place all the ingredients into a blender and blend on high until the sugar is dissolved and the ginger is thoroughly blitzed. Strain through a coffee filter.

Honey syrup

250 g (9 oz) honey
250 ml (8½ fl oz) water

Bring the water to the boil and pour over the honey. Stir well and store in the refrigerator once cooled.

Redcurrant syrup (or *sirop de groseille*)

Follow the grenadine recipe on page 13, using the method that includes the whole seeds.

Kiwi syrup

300 g (10½ oz) kiwi fruit, peeled and diced
250 ml (8½ fl oz) water
250 g (9 oz) sugar

Bring the kiwi fruit and water to a simmer. Simmer for 10 minutes until the water is very green. Strain while hot through a sieve and then through a coffee filter. Add the sugar and whisk or blend to dissolve. Keeps in the fridge for at least 2 weeks.

SHRUBS

Shrubs are old-fashioned cordials where fruit is macerated with vinegar and sugar. The flavour definitely improves after a week or two. They can be stored at room temperature. Feel free to use fruit that is a little past its best or is cosmetically challenged.

Raspberry/blueberry/ strawberry shrub

**125 g (4½ oz) chosen fruit
(coarsely chop strawberries, if using)
85 ml (2¾ fl oz) cider vinegar
(or champagne vinegar)
145 g (5 oz) sugar**

Wash the fruit and put it in a sterilised jar with the vinegar. Cover and let stand for one day. Add the sugar and cover again. Turn the jar over gently to mix and let it stand for several days, turning once a day, until the fruit starts to look a little pale. Strain through a fine-strainer or muslin (cheesecloth) and store in another sterilised jar. The flavour will improve over 2 weeks.

Pineapple shrub

**150 g (5½ oz) peeled pineapple
75 g (2¾ oz) sugar
50 g (1¾ oz) molasses sugar (or molasses)
85 ml (2¾ fl oz) apple cider vinegar**

Mix the ingredients together in a sterilised jar and cover. Turn the jar over gently to mix and let stand for one week, turning once a day. Strain through a fine strainer or muslin (cheesecloth) and store in another sterilised jar. The flavour will improve over 2 weeks.

Martini

The undisputed champion
of prohibition cocktails

◄ ○ ■ ○ ►

'He knows just how I like my martini…full of alcohol.'
Homer Simpson, 2004

At the trial of George Beven in 1928, the jury not only acquitted the suspected bootlegger, they drank all the evidence. When this came to light, they were berated by the magistrate, upon which one of them collapsed and was sent home by the county jail physician.

People say that martinis were mixed with large proportions of vermouth during prohibition to disguise the poor-quality liquor available. Applesauce! Why on earth would anybody who could only afford lousy bathtub gin spend all that *mazuma* on expensive, low-alcohol vermouth?

A COLLECTION OF AROMATIC GIN COCKTAILS

Martini
Cocktail

70 ml (2¼ fl oz) dry gin
2 teaspoons dry vermouth
dash of orange bitters
a brined olive or a twist of
    lemon peel to garnish

Put the first two ingredients into a mixing glass, add plenty of cubed ice and stir gently until the drink is very cold. Strain into a chilled glass and add the bitters and garnish.

Tastes strong and a little aromatic

Arnold Rothstein
Cocktail

60 ml (2 fl oz) dry gin
2 teaspoons dry vermouth
2 teaspoons red vermouth
1 teaspoon Luxardo maraschino liqueur
2 dashes of Angostura bitters
a brined olive, a maraschino cherry and a
    twist of lemon peel on a stick to garnish

Put the first four ingredients into a mixing glass, add plenty of cubed ice and stir gently until the drink is very cold. Strain into a chilled glass and add the bitters and garnish.

Tastes strong, a little sweet and aromatic

Byrrh* cocktail
Cocktail

60 ml (2 fl oz) Old Tom gin
20 ml (¾ fl oz) Byrrh
a twist of lemon peel to garnish

Put the ingredients into a mixing glass, add
plenty of cubed ice and stir gently until the drink
is very cold. Strain into a chilled glass and add
the garnish.

Tastes strong, a little sweet and aromatic

* Pronounced 'beer'

Dance the Charleston at breakfast

Old-fashioned

50 ml (1¾ fl oz) Old Tom gin
30 ml (1 fl oz) Cocchi Vermouth di Torino
1 teaspoon orange marmalade
a twist of orange peel to garnish

Put the ingredients into a shaker, add plenty
of cubed ice and shake until the shaker
is very frosty. Strain into a chilled glass
full of fresh ice and add the garnish.

Tastes sweet and aromatic

Dubonnet cocktail

Cocktail

70 ml (2¼ fl oz) dry gin
2 teaspoons Dubonnet
dash of orange bitters
a twist of lemon peel to garnish

Put the ingredients into a mixing glass,
add plenty of cubed ice and stir gently
until the drink is very cold. Strain into a
chilled glass and add the garnish.

Tastes strong and a little aromatic

Dubonnet deluxe
Cocktail

60 ml (2 fl oz) dry gin
2 teaspoons Dubonnet
2 teaspoons curaçao (or triple sec)
¼ teaspoon absinthe
dash of Boker's bitters (or Angostura bitters)
a twist of lemon peel to garnish

Put the ingredients into a mixing glass, add plenty of cubed ice and stir gently until the drink is very cold. Strain into a chilled glass and add the garnish.

Tastes strong, a little sweet, aromatic and of aniseed

Al Boquerone
Cocktail

50 ml (1¾ fl oz) dry gin
2 teaspoons dry vermouth
2 drops (only!) of Red Boat fish sauce
a brined olive and a boquerone
   on a toothpick to garnish

Put the ingredients into a mixing glass,
add plenty of cubed ice and stir gently
until the drink is very cold. Strain into a
chilled glass and add the garnish.

Tastes strong and a little savoury

Gay divorce
Old-fashioned

30 ml (1 fl oz) Kina l'Aero d'Or
  (or Cocchi Americano)
15 ml (½ fl oz) dry gin
15 ml (½ fl oz) curaçao (or triple sec)
brined olives or a twist of
  lemon peel to garnish

Put the ingredients into a glass, add
plenty of cubed ice and stir gently until
the drink is very cold. Add the garnish.

Tastes sweet, a little strong and aromatic

Four-flusher
Cocktail

40 ml (1¼ fl oz) dry gin
15 ml (½ fl oz) dry vermouth
1 teaspoon Dubonnet
¼ teaspoon absinthe
dash of orange bitters
a twist of orange peel and a
  maraschino cherry to garnish

Put the ingredients into a shaker, add
plenty of cubed ice and shake until
the shaker is very frosty. Strain into a
chilled glass and add the garnish.

Tastes strong, aromatic and a little sweet

Gin cocktail
Old-fashioned

60 ml (2 fl oz) yellow gin (or dry gin)
½ teaspoon curaçao (or triple sec)
½ teaspoon sugar syrup
  (see page 19)
2 dashes of Boker's bitters
  (or Angostura bitters)
a twist of lemon peel to garnish

Fill a glass with cubed ice, add all the ingredients in order and stir gently until it is very cold. Add the garnish to the glass.

Tastes strong and aromatic

Gin julep
Julep cup or Highball

8 mint leaves
2 teaspoons sugar syrup (see page 19)
60 ml (2 fl oz) Old Tom gin (or dry gin)
a mint sprig with a big piece of
  stalk still attached to garnish

Put the first two ingredients into a mixing glass. Using the handle end of a wooden spoon, swirl the leaves around the glass (this will bruise them enough to extract the flavour but not so much as to make them taste like lawn clippings). Fill the serving glass to just over the top with crushed ice and tip this into the mixing glass along with the gin. Stir gently until the glass is frosty. Pour unstrained into the serving glass and stir gently until it is very frosty. Stick the stalk of the garnish way down into the drink.

Tastes strong, sweet and a little aromatic

Monkey's gland cocktail

Old-fashioned

40 ml (1¼ fl oz) dry gin
20 ml (¾ fl oz) fresh orange juice
1 teaspoon absinthe
1 teaspoon homemade grenadine
 (see page 19)
a twist of orange peel to garnish

Put the ingredients into a mixing glass, add plenty of cubed ice and stir gently until the drink is very cold. Strain into a chilled glass and add the garnish.

Tastes sweet and aromatic

GOLD SEAL

ALC

DISTILLED
DRY GIN

90 PROOF

BOTTLED BY

The American Liquor Company

BOSTON

High society dame
Champagne coupe

30 ml (1 fl oz) Old Tom gin
30 ml (1 fl oz) sloe gin
2 dashes of orange bitters
a twist of lemon peel to garnish

Put the ingredients into a mixing glass, add plenty of cubed ice and stir gently until the drink is very cold. Strain into a chilled glass and add the garnish.

Tastes strong, sweet and a little aromatic

Martinez
Champagne coupe

60 ml (2 fl oz) Old Tom gin
40 ml (1¼ fl oz) red vermouth
1 teaspoon Luxardo maraschino liqueur
dash of Boker's bitters (or orange bitters)
a twist of lemon peel to garnish

Put the ingredients into a mixing glass,
add plenty of cubed ice and stir gently
until the drink is very cold. Strain into a
chilled glass and add the garnish.

*Tastes a little strong, sweet and aromatic
(also savoury if garnished with an olive)*

Dry martinez
Champagne coupe

30 ml (1 fl oz) Old Tom gin
30 ml (1 fl oz) dry vermouth
1 teaspoon Luxardo maraschino liqueur
2 dashes of orange bitters
a twist of lemon peel and a
    maraschino cherry to garnish

Put the ingredients into a mixing glass,
add plenty of cubed ice and stir gently
until the drink is very cold. Strain into a
chilled glass and add the garnish.

Tastes a little strong, sweet and aromatic

Old Etonian

Champagne coupe

~~~~~~~~~~~~~~~~~~~~~~

45 ml (1½ fl oz) dry gin
45 ml (1½ fl oz) Kina l'Aero d'Or
   (or Cocchi Americano)
½ teaspoon crème de Noyaux (or amaretto)
2 dashes of orange bitters
a twist of orange peel to garnish

Put the ingredients into a shaker, add
plenty of cubed ice and shake hard until
the shaker is very frosty. Fine-strain into
a chilled glass and add the garnish.

Tastes sweet, bitter and a little aromatic

Cocky American
Cocktail

70 ml (2¼ fl oz) dry gin
2 teaspoons Kina l'Aero d'Or
  (or Cocchi Americano)
a twist of lemon peel to garnish

Put the ingredients into a mixing glass, add plenty of cubed ice and stir gently until the drink is very cold. Strain into a chilled glass and add the garnish.

Tastes strong and a little aromatic

On all sixes
Cocktail

80 ml (2½ fl oz) yellow gin (or other dry gin)
2 teaspoons Swedish punsch
a mint sprig to garnish

Put the ingredients into a mixing glass, add plenty of cubed ice and stir gently until the drink is very cold. Strain into a chilled glass and add the garnish.

Tastes strong and a little sweet

Snorky's kiss
Champagne coupe

40 ml (1¼ fl oz) dry gin
20 ml (¾ fl oz) Byrrh
1 teaspoon crème de cassis
a sprig of blackcurrants to garnish

Put the ingredients into a mixing glass, add plenty of cubed ice and stir gently until the drink is very cold. Strain into a chilled glass and add the garnish.

Tastes strong, a little sweet, bitter and aromatic

Yellow daisy
Cocktail

30 ml (1 fl oz) yellow gin
30 ml (1 fl oz) dry vermouth
15 ml (½ fl oz) curaçao (or triple sec)
½ teaspoon absinthe
a twist of orange peel to garnish

Put the ingredients into a shaker, add plenty of cubed ice and shake hard until the shaker is very frosty. Fine-strain into a chilled glass and add the garnish.

Tastes a little strong, sweet and aromatic

Yellow gin cocktail
Cocktail

70 ml (2¼ fl oz) yellow gin
¼ teaspoon curaçao (or triple sec)
dash of Boker's bitters (or Angostura bitters)
a twist of lemon peel to garnish

Put the first two ingredients into a mixing
glass, add plenty of cubed ice and stir gently
until the drink is very cold. Strain into a chilled
glass and add the bitters and garnish.

Tastes strong and a little aromatic

The cat's pajamas
Cocktail

60 ml (2 fl oz) Plymouth gin
20 ml (¾ fl oz) curaçao (or triple sec)
dash of orange bitters
a twist of orange peel to garnish

Put the first two ingredients into a mixing
glass, add plenty of cubed ice and stir gently
until the drink is very cold. Strain into a chilled
glass and add the bitters and garnish.

Tastes strong, a little sweet and aromatic

New Jersey Turnpike massacre

Champagne coupe

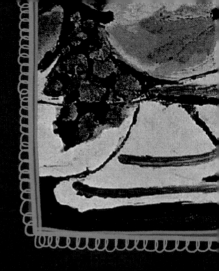

60 ml (2 fl oz) Citadelle Reserve gin (or dry gin)
30 ml (1 fl oz) green chartreuse
a single mint leaf to garnish

Put the ingredients into a shaker, add plenty
of cubed ice and shake hard until the shaker
is very frosty. Fine-strain into a chilled
glass and float the mint leaf on top.

Tastes strong and aromatic

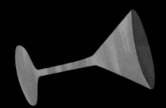

Gibson
Cocktail

70 ml (2¼ fl oz) dry gin
2 teaspoons dry vermouth
a sour cocktail onion on a stick to garnish

Put the ingredients into a mixing
glass, add plenty of cubed ice and stir
gently until the drink is very cold. Strain
into a chilled glass and garnish.

Tastes strong and savoury

Colony cocktail
Cocktail

60 ml (2 fl oz) dry gin
30 ml (1 fl oz) fresh yellow grapefruit juice
2 teaspoons Luxardo maraschino liqueur
a twist of grapefruit peel to garnish

Put the ingredients into a shaker, add
plenty of cubed ice and shake hard until
the shaker is very frosty. Fine-strain into
a chilled glass and add the garnish.

*Tastes a little strong, sour,
sweet and aromatic*

Pink lady
Cocktail

60 ml (2 fl oz) Plymouth gin (or other dry gin)
2 teaspoons homemade grenadine
  (see page 19)
1 egg white
a maraschino cherry and a twist
  of lime peel to garnish

Put the ingredients into a shaker, add plenty of
cubed ice and shake hard for 30 seconds. Fine-
strain into a chilled glass and add the garnish.

Tastes a little creamy, strong and sweet

Theda Bara
Highball

60 ml (2 fl oz) Plymouth gin
30 ml (1 fl oz) unsweetened pomegranate juice
30 ml (1 fl oz) dry vermouth
15 ml (½ fl oz) orange curaçao (or triple sec)
1 teaspoon pomegranate molasses
dash of orange bitters
pomegranate seeds to garnish

Put the ingredients into a mixing glass, add
plenty of cubed ice and stir gently until
the pomegranate molasses is completely
incorporated. Strain into a glass full
of cubed ice and add the garnish.

Tastes a little strong, sweet and sour

Swell gibson
Cocktail

60 ml (2 fl oz) dry gin
2 teaspoons Byrrh
¼ teaspoon sugar syrup (see page 19)
1 brined olive and 2 white cocktail
 onions on a toothpick to garnish

Put the ingredients into a mixing glass,
add plenty of cubed ice and stir gently
until the drink is very cold. Strain into a
chilled glass and add the garnish.

Tastes strong, a little sweet and aromatic

White lily

Cocktail

30 ml (1 fl oz) dry gin
30 ml (1 fl oz) white rum
30 ml (1 fl oz) curaçao (or triple sec)
½ teaspoon absinthe
a slice of orange to garnish

Put the ingredients into a mixing glass,
add plenty of cubed ice and stir gently
until the drink is very cold. Strain into a
chilled glass and add the garnish.

Tastes strong and a little sweet

French 75

*Great literature, great appetites
and a generation lost*

Women made great bootleggers. The social mores of the day, and often
state laws, forbade male police officers or treasury agents from
searching a woman's body, which made way for some very interesting
corsetry. Even having a woman ride along in a bootlegging car meant
that the car was less likely to be stopped.

The French 75 is an enigma; it is refreshing and elegant, yet strong
enough to be named after a 75 mm machine gun used during the
First World War. It was said to be a favourite of dipsomaniacal Lost
Generation types like Hemingway and F. Scott Fitzgerald.

A COLLECTION OF COCKTAILS WHERE CHAMPAGNE IS THE REFRESHING INGREDIENT

French 75

Collins

60 ml (2 fl oz) dry gin
20 ml (¾ fl oz) fresh lemon juice
15 ml (½ fl oz) sugar syrup (see page 19)
approximately 100 ml (3½ fl oz) Brut
  Champagne (or dry sparkling wine)
a slice of lemon to garnish

Put the first three ingredients into a shaker, add
plenty of cubed ice and shake hard until the
shaker is very frosty. Fill a glass halfway with
crushed ice and fine-strain the drink into it. Top
with Champagne and float the garnish on top.

Tastes a little strong, a little sweet and sour

Bloody spats
Cocktail

40 ml (1¼ fl oz) cognac
40 ml (1¼ fl oz) fresh blood orange juice
15 ml (½ fl oz) strawberry liqueur
approximately 30 ml (1 fl oz) Brut
   Champagne (or dry sparkling wine)
a good-looking strawberry to garnish

Put the first three ingredients into a shaker, add plenty of cubed ice and shake hard until the shaker is very frosty. Fill a glass halfway with crushed ice and fine-strain the drink into it. Top with Champagne. Make a slice in the strawberry at the bottom (about 1 cm) and slip it on to the rim of the glass.

Tastes a little strong, sweet and sour

Burra peg
Collins

60 ml (2 fl oz) cognac
2 teaspoons sugar syrup (see page 19)
2 dashes of Angostura bitters
approximately 90 ml (3 fl oz) Brut
   Champagne (or dry sparkling wine)
a twist of orange peel to garnish

Put the first three ingredients into a shaker, add plenty of cubed ice and shake hard until the shaker is very frosty. Fill a glass halfway with crushed ice and fine-strain the drink into it. Top with Champagne and float the garnish on top.

Tastes a little strong and sweet

Champagne cocktail

Champagne coupe or flute

5–10 ml (1–2 teaspoons) sugar
    syrup (see page 19), to taste
dash of Angostura bitters
approximately 140 ml (4½ fl oz) Brut
    Champagne (or dry sparkling wine)
a twist of lemon peel to garnish

Put the first two ingredients into a glass then
pour in the chilled Champagne. Stir very briefly
to incorporate the sugar and add the garnish.

Tastes bubbly, delightful and a little sweet

CUVÉE BRUT
1923
Mademoiselle
CHAMPAGNE

Half Eton breakfast
Champagne flute (for 2)

45 ml (1½ fl oz) dry gin
45 ml (1½ fl oz) Kina l'Aero d'Or
   (or Cocchi Americano)
½ teaspoon crème de Noyaux (or amaretto)
2 dashes of orange bitters
2 teaspoons fresh lemon juice
approximately 200 ml (7 fl oz) Brut
   Champagne (or dry sparkling wine)
a twist of orange peel for each
   glass to garnish

Put the first five ingredients into a shaker,
add plenty of cubed ice and shake hard
until the shaker is very frosty. Fine-strain,
dividing evenly between two glasses, top
with Champagne and add the garnish.

Tastes a little strong, sweet, bitter and sour

Colony royale
Champagne coupe

60 ml (2 fl oz) Plymouth gin
30 ml (1 fl oz) fresh yellow grapefruit juice
1 teaspoon Luxardo maraschino liqueur
approximately 90 ml (3 fl oz) Brut
   Champagne (or dry sparkling wine)
a twist of grapefruit peel to garnish

Put the first three ingredients into a shaker, add
plenty of cubed ice and shake hard until the
shaker is very frosty. Fine-strain into a glass.
Top with Champagne and add the garnish.

Tastes a little strong, sweet and sour

King's peg
Collins

60 ml (2 fl oz) cognac
20 ml (¾ fl oz) fresh lemon juice
15 ml (½ fl oz) sugar syrup (see page 19)
approximately 100 ml (3½ fl oz)
   Brut Champagne (or dry sparkling wine)
a slice of orange to garnish

Put the first three ingredients into a shaker, add
plenty of cubed ice and shake hard until the
shaker is very frosty. Fill a glass halfway with
crushed ice and fine-strain the drink into it. Top
with Champagne and float the garnish on top.

Tastes a little strong, sweet and sour

Death in the afternoon

Champagne flute

30 ml (1 fl oz) absinthe
1 teaspoon curaçao (or triple sec)
approximately 120 ml (4 fl oz) Brut
   Champagne (or dry sparkling wine)

Put the first two ingredients into a glass,
add the Champagne slowly and mix once.

Tastes strong, sweet and of aniseed

Southside royale

Collins

60 ml (2 fl oz) dry gin
20 ml (¾ fl oz) fresh lemon juice
15 ml (½ fl oz) sugar syrup (see page 19)
4–6 mint leaves
approximately 100 ml (3½ fl oz) Brut
   Champagne (or dry sparkling wine)
a mint sprig to garnish

Put the first four ingredients into a shaker, add
plenty of cubed ice and shake hard until the
shaker is very frosty. Fill a glass halfway with
crushed ice and fine-strain the drink into it. Top
with Champagne and float the garnish on top.

Tastes a little strong, sweet and sour

Let's blouse
Champagne flute

40 ml (1¼ fl oz) white rum
20 ml (¾ fl oz) strawberry shrub (see page 21)
approximately 80 ml (2½ fl oz)
   Brut Champagne (or dry sparkling wine)
brined olives or a twist of
   lemon peel to garnish

Put the first two ingredients into a mixing glass,
add plenty of cubed ice and stir gently until the
drink is very cold. Strain into a chilled glass,
top with Champagne and add the garnish.

Tastes refreshing, a little sweet and sour

Live wire
Champagne flute

30 ml (1 fl oz) absinthe
30 ml (1 fl oz) green crème de menthe
approximately 60 ml (2 fl oz) Brut
   Champagne (or dry sparkling wine)
a good-looking star anise and
   a mint leaf to garnish

Put the first two ingredients into a mixing
glass, add plenty of cubed ice and stir
gently until the drink is very cold. Strain
into a glass, add the Champagne slowly
and mix once before adding the garnish.

Tastes strong, sweet, minty and of aniseed

Morning glory royale
Champagne coupe

30 ml (1 fl oz) Scotch whisky (or rye whiskey)
30 ml (1 fl oz) cognac
2 teaspoons curaçao (or triple sec)
1 teaspoon sugar syrup (see page 19)
½ teaspoon absinthe
2 dashes of orange bitters
approximately 30 ml (1 fl oz) Brut
   Champagne (or dry sparkling wine)
a twist of orange peel to garnish

Put the first six ingredients into a mixing glass, add plenty of cubed ice and stir gently until the drink is very cold. Strain into a chilled glass, top with Champagne and add the garnish.

Tastes a little sweet, sour and aromatic

Old Cuban
Champagne flute

60 ml (2 fl oz) dark rum
30 ml (1 fl oz) fresh lime juice
2 teaspoons sugar syrup (see page 19)
4 mint leaves
dash of Angostura bitters
dash of orange bitters
approximately 60 ml (2 fl oz) Brut
   Champagne (or dry sparkling wine)
a twist of lime peel to garnish

Put the first six ingredients into a shaker, add plenty of cubed ice and shake until the shaker is very frosty. Strain into a chilled glass, top with Champagne and add the garnish.

Tastes strong, a little sour and aromatic

St Valentine's Day massacre

Collins

45 ml (1½ fl oz) Scotch whisky
30 ml (1 fl oz) white rum
15 g (½ oz) good-quality quince jelly
approximately 90 ml (3 fl oz) Brut
    Champagne (or dry sparkling wine)
a piece of poached quince or a twist
    of orange peel to garnish

Put the first three ingredients into a shaker, add
plenty of cubed ice and shake hard until the
shaker is very frosty. Fill a glass halfway with
crushed ice and fine-strain the drink into it. Top
with Champagne and float the garnish on top.

Tastes sweet and a little strong

Seelbach

Champagne flute

30 ml (1 fl oz) bourbon (or rye whiskey)
15 ml (½ fl oz) curaçao (or triple sec)
100–120 ml (3½–4 fl oz) Brut
   Champagne (or dry sparkling wine)
4 dashes of Angostura bitters
4 dashes of Peychaud's bitters
a twist of lemon peel to garnish

Put the first two ingredients into a mixing
glass, add plenty of cubed ice and stir
gently until the drink is very cold. Strain
into a glass and add the Champagne,
both the bitters and the garnish.

Tastes strong, a little sweet and aromatic

Says you!

Champagne flute

30 ml (1 fl oz) Scotch whisky
2 teaspoons pineapple shrub (see page 21)
approximately 70 ml (2¼ fl oz) Brut
    Champagne (or dry sparkling wine)
a small wedge of pineapple with
    the skin on to garnish

Put the first two ingredients into a mixing glass,
add plenty of cubed ice and stir gently until the
drink is very cold. Strain into a chilled glass and
top with Champagne. Cut a slice into the wedge
of pineapple and fix it to the rim of the glass.

Tastes refreshing, a little sweet and sour

Tommy gun*
Highball

15 ml (½ fl oz) dark rum
15 ml (½ fl oz) white rum
15 ml (½ fl oz) dry gin
15 ml (½ fl oz) cognac
15 ml (½ fl oz) Canadian whisky
15 ml (½ fl oz) rye whiskey
15 ml (½ fl oz) Scotch whisky
15 ml (½ fl oz) Luxardo maraschino liqueur
1 teaspoon fresh lemon juice
dash of orange bitters
approximately 90 ml (3 fl oz) Brut
  Champagne (or dry sparkling wine)
a slice of orange to garnish

Put the first ten ingredients into a shaker, add
plenty of cubed ice and shake until the shaker
is very frosty. Strain into a chilled glass, top
with Champagne and add the garnish.

Tastes a little strong and sweet

*A fast killer with very little recoil.

Bacardi

The rush to Havana and the rum lovers

◄ ◉■◉ ►

During prohibition, American drinkers and bartenders alike
flocked to Cuba in their thousands to drink and make drinks legally.
There they discovered exotic cocktails made with the local rum
like the daiquiri and the mojito. The famously sloshed
Ernest Hemingway, a regular visitor to Cuba, managed to
consume a record sixteen of his special daiquiris called the
Papa doble in one night. That's just shy of three whole bottles of rum!
Back in the speakeasies of the States, the sugar in the daiquiri
was replaced with grenadine and the bacardi cocktail was born.

A COLLECTION OF RUM-BASED COCKTAILS

Bacardi cocktail
Cocktail

80 ml (2½ fl oz) Bacardi white rum
20 ml (¾ fl oz) fresh lime juice
2–4 teaspoons homemade grenadine*
  (see page 19)
a slice of lime to garnish

METHOD 1
Put the ingredients into a shaker, add plenty
of cubed ice and shake until the shaker is
very frosty. Strain into a chilled glass and
fix the garnish to the rim of the glass.

METHOD 2
Put the ingredients into a blender, add
200 g (7 oz) cubed ice and blend until the
drink is smooth and looks like a slushy.
Pour unstrained into a chilled glass and
fix the garnish to the rim of the glass.

*Tastes strong, sour and, if you use
4 teaspoons of grenadine, sweet*

*If you're looking for a proper sour, use
 2 teaspoons; if you aren't sweet enough,
 use 4 teaspoons.

A real rumdinger
Cocktail

60 ml (2 fl oz) dark rum
15 ml (½ fl oz) crème de Noyaux (or amaretto)
1 teaspoon Cocchi Vermouth di Torino
a twist of lemon peel to garnish

Put the ingredients into a shaker, add
plenty of cubed ice and shake hard until
the shaker is very frosty. Fine-strain into
a chilled glass and add the garnish.

Tastes strong, sweet and a little aromatic

Bam! Right on the kisser

Champagne coupe

~~~~~~~~~~~~~~~~~~~~~~~~~~~~~~~~~~

30 ml (1 fl oz) white rum
30 ml (1 fl oz) Kina l'Aero d'Or
   (or Cocchi Americano)
2 teaspoons fresh lime juice
1 teaspoon homemade grenadine
   (see page 19)
a twist of lime peel to garnish

Put the ingredients into a mixing glass,
add plenty of cubed ice and stir gently
until the drink is very cold. Strain into a
chilled glass and add the garnish.

*Tastes sweet, aromatic, a little sour
and bitter*

Fast boat to Kingston
Cocktail

80 ml (2½ fl oz) dark rum
20 ml (¾ fl oz) crème de
   pamplemousse rosé
20 ml (¾ fl oz) fresh lime juice
a twist of ruby grapefruit peel to garnish

Put the ingredients into a mixing glass,
add plenty of cubed ice and stir gently
until the drink is very cold. Strain into a
chilled glass and add the garnish.

Tastes strong, sweet and sour

Half-seas over
Highball

120 ml (4 fl oz) dark rum
40 ml (1¼ fl oz) fresh lime juice
30 ml (1 fl oz) homemade
   grenadine (see page 19)
a slice of lime to garnish

Put the ingredients into a shaker, add plenty
of cubed ice and shake hard until the shaker
is very frosty. Fine-strain into a chilled glass
full of fresh ice and float the garnish on top.

Tastes strong and sweet

Mary Pickford
Cocktail

60 ml (2 fl oz) white rum
50 ml (1¾ fl oz) unsweetened pineapple juice
1 teaspoon homemade grenadine
   (see page 19)
½ teaspoon Luxardo maraschino liqueur
a maraschino cherry to garnish

Put the ingredients into a shaker, add
plenty of cubed ice and shake hard until
the shaker is very frosty. Fine-strain into
a chilled glass and add the garnish.

Tastes strong, sweet and a little sour

American bartender heads south

Cocktail

60 ml (2 fl oz) dark rum
15 ml (½ fl oz) Cocchi Vermouth di Torino
dash of orange bitters
a twist of orange peel to garnish

Put the first two ingredients into a mixing glass, add plenty of cubed ice and stir gently until the drink is very cold. Strain into a chilled glass and add the bitters and garnish.

Tastes strong, aromatic and a little sweet

Millionaire cocktail

Champagne coupe

15 ml (½ fl oz) dark rum
15 ml (½ fl oz) sloe gin
15 ml (½ fl oz) apricot brandy
15 ml (½ fl oz) fresh lime juice
½ teaspoon homemade grenadine
  (see page 19)

Put the ingredients into a mixing glass, add
plenty of cubed ice and stir gently until the drink
is very cold. Strain into a chilled glass.

Tastes a little strong, sweet and sour

'Pappy' Chalk*
Cocktail

30 ml (1 fl oz) Swedish punsch
15 ml (½ fl oz) Old Bahamian
 rum (or other dark rum)
15 ml (½ fl oz) Kina l'Aero d'Or
 (or Cocchi Americano)
15 ml (½ fl oz) fresh lime juice
a slice of lime to garnish

Put the ingredients into a mixing glass,
add plenty of cubed ice and stir gently
until the drink is very cold. Strain into a
chilled glass and add the garnish.

Tastes sweet, sour, a little strong and bitter

*Returned WWI pilot Arthur 'Pappy' Chalk began the
world's first commercial international flight route
between Fort Lauderdale and the Bahamas in 1917.
During prohibition, Pappy became a major importer of
Bahamian rum.

Planter's cocktail
Cocktail

60 ml (2 fl oz) dark rum
30 ml (1 fl oz) fresh lime juice
2 teaspoons sugar syrup (see page 19)
a slice of lime to garnish

Put the ingredients into a shaker, add plenty
of cubed ice and shake hard until the shaker
is very frosty. Fine-strain into a chilled glass and
add the garnish.

Tastes strong, sour and a little sweet

Rum shrub
Collins

30 ml (1 fl oz) white rum
30 ml (1 fl oz) dark rum
30 ml (1 fl oz) pineapple shrub (see page 21)
soda water (club soda)
a slice of lime to garnish

Put the first three ingredients into a shaker, add
plenty of cubed ice and shake until the shaker is
very frosty. Strain into a chilled glass, top with
soda water and add the garnish.

Tastes refreshing, sweet and a little sour

Planter's punch
Punch bowl (serves 10)

600 ml (20½ fl oz) dark rum
400 ml (13½ fl oz) sugar syrup (see page 19)
200 ml (7 fl oz) fresh lime juice
200 ml (7 fl oz) soda water (club soda)
sliced pineapple, lime, orange
  and mint to garnish

Put the first three ingredients into the punch
bowl, add plenty of cubed ice and stir gently
until the drink is very cold. Add the soda
water, stir once, then add the fruit and mint.

Tastes refreshing, deceptively so!

Papa doble*
Cocktail

120 ml (4 fl oz) white rum
30 ml (1 fl oz) fresh lime juice
30 ml (1 fl oz) fresh yellow grapefruit juice
½ teaspoon Luxardo maraschino liqueur
200 g (7 oz) cubed ice

Put the ingredients into a blender
and blend until the drink has a fluffy
texture. Pour unstrained into a glass.

Tastes strong and sour

*Even though this drink is delicious, please don't
  drink sixteen in a row like Hemingway did!

Presidente
Champagne coupe

45 ml (1½ fl oz) white rum
45 ml (1½ fl oz) dry vermouth
20 ml (¾ fl oz) curaçao (or triple sec)
1 teaspoon homemade grenadine
    (see page 19)
brined olives or a twist of
    lemon peel to garnish

Put the ingredients into a mixing glass,
add plenty of cubed ice and stir gently
until the drink is very cold. Strain into a
chilled glass and add the garnish.

Tastes strong and a little aromatic

Mazuma
Cocktail

30 ml (1 fl oz) white rum
30 ml (1 fl oz) Swedish punsch
15 ml (½ fl oz) fresh lime juice
150 g (5½ oz) cubed ice

Put the ingredients into a blender
and blend until the drink has a fluffy
texture. Pour unstrained into a glass.

Tastes refreshing, a little sour and aromatic

Not quite No. 3 daiquiri
Cocktail

60 ml (2 fl oz) white rum
15 ml (½ fl oz) fresh lime juice
1½ teaspoons Luxardo maraschino liqueur
200 g (7 oz) cubed ice

Put the ingredients into a blender and blend until the drink has a fluffy texture. Pour unstrained into a glass*.

Tastes refreshing, sour and a little strong

*This recipe makes a dry cocktail; you can add up to 15 ml (½ fl oz) of sugar syrup (see page 19) if it's too sour.

The lovely unrefined daiquiri
Cocktail

60 ml (2 fl oz) white rum
15 ml (½ fl oz) fresh lime juice
1 teaspoon sugar

Put the ingredients into a shaker with crushed ice and shake hard for 30 seconds or until the shaker is very frosty. Strain into a glass using a hawthorne strainer*; you want shards of ice and little bits of undissolved sugar to make it into the drink.

Tastes refreshing, sour and a little strong

* A hawthorne strainer is a flat metal strainer with a wire coil around the edge that fits into a cocktail shaker.

Daiquiri
Cocktail

60 ml (2 fl oz) white rum
15 ml (½ fl oz) fresh lime juice
1½ teaspoons sugar syrup (see page 19)
200 g (7 oz) ice

Put the ingredients into a blender and
blend until the drink has a fluffy texture.
Pour unstrained into a glass*.

Tastes refreshing, sour and a little strong

*This recipe makes a dry cocktail; you can add
another 15 ml (½ fl oz) of sugar syrup if it's too sour.

Mojito
Collins

~~~~~~~~~~~~~~~~~~~~~~~~~~~~~~~~~~

2 teaspoons sugar syrup (see page 19)
10 mint leaves*
60 ml (2 fl oz) white rum
20 ml (¾ fl oz) fresh lime juice
a spent lime shell** to garnish
soda water (club soda)
a sprig of mint to garnish

Put the first two ingredients into a glass. Using
the handle end of a wooden spoon, swirl the
leaves around the glass (this will bruise them
enough to extract the flavour but not so much
as to make them taste like lawn clippings).
Add the rum and lime juice, and fill the glass
with cubed ice, stirring until the glass is frosty.
Push the lime shell into the drink, top with
soda, stir once and float the mint sprig on top.

Tastes strong and a little aromatic

*Spearmint is more authentic than peppermint for this
drink, but peppermint has a more vibrant flavour.

**Half a lime after the juice has been squeezed out.

Puppet dictator
Julep cup or Highball

8 fresh pineapple sage leaves*
2 teaspoons sugar syrup (see page 19)
60 ml (2 fl oz) dark rum
a sprig of pineapple sage to garnish

Put the first two ingredients into a mixing glass. Using the handle end of a wooden spoon, swirl the leaves around the glass (this will bruise them enough to extract the flavour but not so much as to make them taste like lawn clippings). Fill the serving glass to just over the top with crushed ice and tip this into the mixing glass along with the rum. Stir gently until the glass is frosty. Pour unstrained into the serving glass, stir gently until it is very frosty then add the garnish.

Tastes strong, sweet and a little aromatic

*Don't let this drink stand for too long or the pineapple sage leaves will start to make the drink bitter.

Take the nickel
Cocktail

30 ml (1 fl oz) white rum
30 ml (1 fl oz) Kina l'Aero d'Or
  (or Cocchi Americano)
30 ml (1 fl oz) crème de pamplemousse rosé
30 ml (1 fl oz) fresh lime juice
a twist of lime peel to garnish

Put the ingredients into a mixing glass, add plenty of cubed ice and stir gently until the drink is very cold. Strain into a chilled glass and add the garnish.

Tastes sweet, sour, a little strong and bitter

The metropolis
Cocktail or Old-fashioned

~~~~~~~~~~~~~~~~~~~~~~~~~~~~~~~~~~

50 ml (1¾ fl oz) dark rum
40 ml (1¼ fl oz) red vermouth
1 teaspoon curaçao (or triple sec)
dash of Peychaud's bitters
a maraschino cherry to garnish

Put the ingredients into a mixing glass,
add plenty of cubed ice and stir gently until
the drink is very cold. Strain into a chilled
glass (if using an old-fashioned glass add
more cubed ice) and add the garnish.

Tastes strong, a little sweet and aromatic

The cullross
Cocktail

30 ml (1 fl oz) white rum
30 ml (1 fl oz) Kina l'Aero d'Or
  (or Cocchi Americano)
30 ml (1 fl oz) apricot brandy
2 teaspoons fresh lemon juice
a twist of orange peel to garnish

Put the ingredients into a mixing glass,
add plenty of cubed ice and stir gently
until the drink is very cold. Strain into a
chilled glass and add the garnish.

Tastes a little strong, sweet, sour and bitter

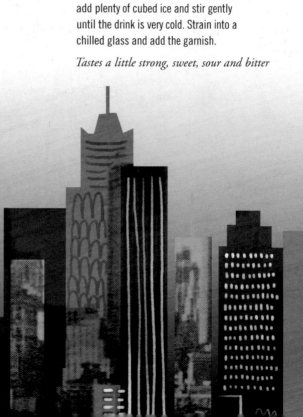

Jack Rose

A bathtub full of deceit

Applejack is not distilled. You just fill a bathtub with apple juice, add a bit of yeast, let it brew for a few weeks and then leave it out in the winter to freeze. The lower the temperature, the more booze in the unfrozen part. Ironically, bathtub gin wasn't made in bathtubs, but the bottles it was made in were so tall they needed to be filled up in the bathtub.

'Baldy Jack Rose' was a double-crossing gambler and Jewish underworld figure in New York who quite probably got away with murder by selling his police captain crime boss up the river. The *Jack Rose* wasn't named after him, but his story is a cool one.

A COLLECTION OF APPLEJACK AND CALVADOS COCKTAILS

Jack Rose

Champagne coupe

60 ml (2 fl oz) calvados (or applejack)
15 ml (½ fl oz) fresh lime juice
2 teaspoons homemade grenadine
 (see page 19)
a slice of lime to garnish

Put the ingredients into a shaker, add
plenty of cubed ice and shake hard until
the shaker is very frosty. Fine-strain into a
chilled glass and float the garnish on top.

*Tastes fruity, sour, a little sweet
and strong*

Eton an apple

Cocktail

~~~~~~~~~~~~~~~~~~~~~~~~~~~~~~~~~~

45 ml (1½ fl oz) calvados (or applejack)
45 ml (1½ fl oz) Kina l'Aero d'Or
  (or Cocchi Americano)
1 teaspoon crème de Noyaux (or amaretto)
dash of orange bitters
a twist of orange peel to garnish

Put the ingredients into a mixing glass,
add plenty of cubed ice and stir gently
until the drink is very cold. Strain into a
chilled glass and add the garnish.

Tastes strong, sweet and a little bitter

Scofflaw

Cocktail

~~~~~~~~~~~~~~~~~~~~~~~~~~~~~~~~~~

60 ml (2 fl oz) calvados (or applejack)
1 teaspoon crème de Noyaux (or amaretto)
1 teaspoon curaçao (or triple sec)
30 ml (1 fl oz) apple juice,
  preferably cold-pressed
a twist of lemon peel to garnish

Put the ingredients into a mixing glass,
add plenty of cubed ice and stir gently
until the drink is very cold. Strain into a
chilled glass and add the garnish.

Tastes appley, strong and a little sweet

High hat
Old-fashioned

30 ml (1 fl oz) calvados (or applejack)
15 ml (½ fl oz) Swedish punsch
15 ml (½ fl oz) Campari
a twist of orange peel to garnish

Put the ingredients in a mixing glass, add plenty of cubed ice and stir gently until the drink is very cold. Strain into a chilled glass full of fresh cubed ice and add the garnish.

Tastes strong, sweet and bitter

Road to hell paved with unbought stuffed dogs

Old-fashioned

15 ml (½ fl oz) calvados (or applejack)
15 ml (½ fl oz) dark Jamaican
 rum (or other aged rum)
15 ml (½ fl oz) Byrrh
dash of Peychaud's bitters
the prettiest star anise you can find and
 a twist of mandarin peel to garnish

Put the ingredients into a glass, add
plenty of cubed ice and stir gently until
the drink is very cold. Add the garnish.

Tastes strong, a little sweet and aromatic

Foreign correspondent

Champagne coupe

30 ml (1 fl oz) calvados (or applejack)
15 ml (½ fl oz) D.O.M. Benedictine
15 ml (½ fl oz) fresh lime juice
a slice of lime to garnish

Put the ingredients into a mixing glass,
add plenty of cubed ice and stir gently
until the drink is very cold. Strain into a
chilled glass and add the garnish.

Tastes sweet, a little strong and sour

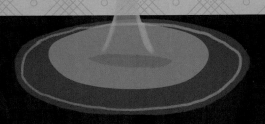

The song of the prune

Champagne coupe

30 ml (1 fl oz) calvados (or applejack)
30 ml (1 fl oz) sloe gin
½ teaspoon crème de Noyaux (or amaretto)
2 drops only of Angostura bitters
a prune to garnish

Put the ingredients into a mixing glass,
add plenty of cubed ice and stir gently
until the drink is very cold. Strain into a
chilled glass and add the garnish.

Tastes a little strong, sweet and sour

Rich daddy
Old-fashioned

45 ml (1½ fl oz) calvados (or applejack)
15 ml (½ fl oz) Kina l'Aero d'Or
  (or Cocchi Americano)
1 teaspoon clove syrup (see page 20)
a twist of lemon peel to garnish

Put the ingredients into a mixing glass, add plenty of cubed ice and stir gently until the drink is very cold. Strain into a chilled glass full of fresh cubed ice and add the garnish.

Tastes sweet, aromatic, a little strong and bitter

Twelve miles out
Cocktail

30 ml (1 fl oz) calvados (or applejack)
30 ml (1 fl oz) white rum
30 ml (1 fl oz) Swedish punsch
a small wedge of pineapple with
   the skin on to garnish

Put the ingredients into a mixing glass,
add plenty of cubed ice and stir gently
until the drink is very cold. Strain into a
chilled glass. Cut a slice into the wedge of
pineapple and fix it to the rim of the glass.

Tastes strong, sweet and a little aromatic

Manhattan

The leaky northern border

◄◦■◦►

It is estimated that during prohibition, 75 per cent of all
booze in the States came in over the Detroit River.

Through the Mexico Export Company, big-time bootleggers like
'King Canada' sent small boats laden with Canadian Club to places
like 'Barbados' and 'Mexico' where booze was legal. Of course, Mexico
and Barbados had plenty of booze, so the boats wouldn't actually travel
more than a mile across the river to Detroit. No one on the Canadian
side seemed to raise an eyebrow when a small boat seemed to make
the 4,000 kilometre round trip to the Caribbean three times a day!

Canadian whisky was so popular that it came to replace rye whiskey as the primary
ingredient in a Manhattan, even as far from the yoke of prohibition as London.

A COLLECTION OF WHISKEY-BASED COCKTAILS

Perfect Manhattan

Cocktail or old-fashioned

45 ml (1½ fl oz) Canadian
   whisky (or rye whiskey)
15 ml (½ fl oz) dry vermouth
2 teaspoons red vermouth
dash of orange bitters
a maraschino cherry and a twist
   of orange peel to garnish

Put the ingredients into a mixing glass, add
plenty of cubed ice and stir gently until
the drink is very cold. Strain into a chilled
glass (if using an old-fashioned glass add
more cubed ice) and add the garnish.

Tastes strong, a little sweet and aromatic

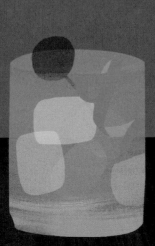

8 OVER YEARS OLD   8 OVER YEARS OLD

RIVERBOAT RYE

Bourbon Manhattan

Cocktail or Old-fashioned

60 ml (2 fl oz) syrupy bourbon such as Maker's
   Mark or Bulleit
15 ml (½ fl oz) Cocchi Vermouth Di Torino
dash of orange bitters
a twist of orange peel and maraschino
   cherry to garnish

Put the ingredients into a mixing glass, add
plenty of cubed ice and stir gently until the drink
is very cold. Strain into a chilled glass (if using
an old-fashioned glass add more cubed ice) and
add the garnish.

Tastes strong, aromatic and a little sweet

Beer Manhattan

Cocktail

60 ml (2 fl oz) bourbon
15 ml (½ fl oz) Byrrh
a twist of orange peel and a
   maraschino cherry to garnish

Put the ingredients into a mixing glass,
add plenty of cubed ice and stir gently
until the drink is very cold. Strain into a
chilled glass and add the garnish.

Tastes strong and a little aromatic

Millionaire cocktail 2

Cocktail

60 ml (2 fl oz) rye whiskey
15 ml (½ fl oz) curaçao (or triple sec)
2 teaspoons fresh lemon juice
1 teaspoon homemade grenadine
  (see page 19)
½ teaspoon absinthe
1 egg white
a twist of lemon peel to garnish

Put the ingredients into a shaker, add
plenty of cubed ice and shake hard until
the shaker is very frosty. Fine-strain into
a chilled glass and add the garnish.

Tastes a little creamy, strong,
sweet, sour and of aniseed

'Lucky' Luciano

Old-fashioned

60 ml (2 fl oz) rye whiskey
  (or Canadian whisky)
60 ml (2 fl oz) fresh blood orange juice
1 teaspoon homemade grenadine
  (see page 19)
2 dashes of orange bitters
a twist of blood orange peel to garnish

Put the ingredients into a mixing glass, add
plenty of cubed ice and stir gently until the
drink is very cold. Strain into a chilled glass
full of fresh cubed ice and add the garnish.

Tastes a little strong, sweet and sour

Bimbo

Old-fashioned

60 ml (2 fl oz) Scotch whisky
15 ml (½ fl oz) Cocchi Vermouth di Torino
1 teaspoon Luxardo maraschino liqueur
dash of orange bitters
a twist of orange peel to garnish

Put the ingredients into a mixing glass, add
plenty of cubed ice and stir gently until the
drink is very cold. Strain into a chilled glass
full of fresh cubed ice and add the garnish.

Tastes strong, sweet and aromatic

Blood and sand
Cocktail

20 ml (¾ fl oz) Scotch whisky
20 ml (¾ fl oz) cherry brandy (or Guignolet)
20 ml (¾ fl oz) red vermouth (preferably
   Cocchi Vermouth di Torino)
20 ml (¾ fl oz) fresh orange juice
dash of orange bitters
a twist of orange peel to garnish

Put the ingredients into a mixing glass,
add plenty of cubed ice and stir gently
until the drink is very cold. Strain into a
chilled glass and add the garnish.

Tastes a little strong, sweet and aromatic

Bobby Burns
Cocktail

30 ml (1 fl oz) Scotch whisky
30 ml (1 fl oz) red vermouth
1 teaspoon D.O.M. Benedictine
a twist of lemon peel to garnish

Put the ingredients into a mixing glass,
add plenty of cubed ice and stir gently
until the drink is very cold. Strain into a
chilled glass and add the garnish.

Tastes strong, sweet and aromatic

In a pickle
Cocktail

60 ml (2 fl oz) Scotch whisky
20 ml (¾ fl oz) Dubonnet
2 teaspoons pickle brine*
1 teaspoon clove syrup (see page 20)
dash of orange bitters
a brined olive and a slice of pickle
   on a toothpick to garnish

Put the ingredients into a mixing glass,
add plenty of cubed ice and stir gently
until the drink is very cold. Strain into a
chilled glass and add the garnish.

Tastes strong, a little savoury and sweet

*Make sure you choose brined pickles
(i.e. no vinegar or sugar).

Hayburner
Champagne coupe

40 ml (1¼ fl oz) Canadian whisky
20 ml (¾ fl oz) green chartreuse
dash of orange bitters
a twist of orange peel to garnish

Put the ingredients into a shaker, add
plenty of cubed ice and shake hard until
the shaker is very frosty. Fine-strain into
a chilled glass and add the garnish.

Tastes strong, aromatic and a little sweet

Chocolate Sazerac
Old-fashioned

60 ml (2 fl oz) rye whiskey
2 teaspoons crème de cacao
dash of Peychaud's bitters
¼ teaspoon absinthe
a twist of orange peel to garnish

Put the first three ingredients into a mixing glass, add plenty of cubed ice and stir gently until the drink is very cold. Meanwhile, put the absinthe into a chilled glass and turn it gently to coat the inside. Strain the contents of the mixing glass into the prepared glass and add the garnish.

Tastes strong, a little sweet, aromatic and of aniseed

Buried in clover
Old-fashioned

70 ml (2¼ fl oz) Canadian whisky
2 teaspoons clove syrup (see page 20)
dash of Angostura bitters
a slice of orange studded with
   3 whole cloves to garnish

Put the first two ingredients into a mixing glass, add plenty of cubed ice and stir gently until the drink is very cold. Strain into a chilled glass full of fresh cubed ice and add the bitters and garnish.

Tastes strong, sweet and aromatic

Detroit River crossing
Cocktail

~~~~~~~~~~~~~~~~~~~~~~~~~~~~~~

60 ml (2 fl oz) Canadian whisky
2 teaspoons curaçao (or triple sec)
2 dashes of orange bitters
a twist of orange peel to garnish

Put the ingredients into a mixing glass,
add plenty of cubed ice and stir gently
until the drink is very cold. Strain into a
chilled glass and add the garnish.

*Tastes strong, orangey, a little
sweet and aromatic*

Ginger cocktail
Old-fashioned

~~~~~~~~~~~~~~~~~~~~~~~~~~~~~~

70 ml (2¼ fl oz) Canadian whisky
2 teaspoons ginger syrup (see page 20)
2 dashes of orange bitters
a piece of candied (crystallized)
    ginger and a slice of fresh ginger
    on a toothpick to garnish

Put the first two ingredients into a mixing
glass, add plenty of cubed ice and stir
gently until the drink is very cold. Strain
into a chilled glass full of fresh cubed
ice and add the bitters and garnish.

Tastes strong, sweet and pungent

Hard boiled
Champagne coupe

30 ml (1 fl oz) bourbon or rye whiskey
15 ml (½ fl oz) green chartreuse

Put the ingredients into a mixing glass, add plenty of cubed ice and stir gently until the drink is very cold. Strain into a chilled glass.

Tastes strong, sweet and a little aromatic

Whiskey sour
Cocktail or Old-fashioned

60 ml (2 fl oz) rye whiskey
  (or Canadian whisky)
20 ml (¾ fl oz) fresh lemon juice
2 teaspoons sugar syrup (see page 19)
a slice of lemon to garnish

Put the ingredients into a mixing glass, add
plenty of cubed ice and stir gently until
the drink is very cold. Strain into a chilled
glass (if using an old-fashioned glass add
more cubed ice) and add the garnish*.

Tastes strong and a little aromatic

*You can add an egg white to this drink. If you
do, shake it and serve in a cocktail glass.

Making whoopee became all the rage
Champagne coupe

45 ml (1½ fl oz) Canadian whisky
15 ml (½ fl oz) dry vermouth
1 teaspoon crème de cacao
dash of Angostura bitters
a piece of chocolate-dipped candied
  (crystallized) orange to garnish

Put the ingredients into a mixing glass,
add plenty of cubed ice and stir gently until
the drink is very cold. Strain into a chilled
glass. Using a knife, put a small slice in the
garnish and fix it to the rim of the glass.

Tastes strong, sweet and aromatic

Mexico export company

Cocktail

~~~~~~~~~~~~~~~~~~~~~~~~

50 ml (1¾ fl oz) Canadian whisky
2 teaspoons dark rum
2 teaspoons fresh lime juice
1 teaspoon ginger syrup (see page 20)
1 teaspoon clove syrup (see page 20)
dash of orange bitters
a twist of lime peel to garnish

Put the ingredients into a mixing glass,
add plenty of cubed ice and stir gently
until the drink is very cold. Strain into a
chilled glass and add the garnish.

*Tastes strong, sweet, a little
aromatic and sour*

On the lam

Champagne coupe

60 ml (2 fl oz) Canadian whisky
30 ml (1 fl oz) absinthe
1 teaspoon clove syrup (see page 20)
a twist of grapefruit peel to garnish

Put the ingredients into a shaker, add
plenty of cubed ice and shake until
the shaker is very frosty. Strain into a
chilled glass and add the garnish.

*Tastes strong, sweet, of aniseed,
and a little aromatic*

Monkey's chatter
Cocktail

45 ml (1½ fl oz) Canadian whisky
15 ml (½ fl oz) blueberry shrub (see page 21)
1 teaspoon homemade grenadine
  (see page 18)
½ teaspoon dry vermouth
dash of orange bitters
fresh blueberries to garnish

Put the ingredients in a mixing glass, add plenty of cubed ice and stir gently until the drink is very cold. Strain into a chilled glass and add the garnish.

Tastes strong, sweet, a little sour and aromatic

On a toot
Old-fashioned

30 ml (1 fl oz) Scotch whisky
15 ml (½ fl oz) Byrrh
1 teaspoon Luxardo maraschino liqueur
dash of orange bitters
a twist of orange peel to garnish

Put the ingredients into a glass, add plenty of cubed ice and stir gently until the drink is very cold. Add the garnish.

Tastes strong, sweet and bitter

Original gangster
Cocktail

60 ml (2 fl oz) bourbon
15 ml (½ fl oz) Luxardo maraschino liqueur
20 ml (¾ fl oz) fresh Meyer lemon juice
  (or 15 ml (½ fl oz) fresh lemon juice)
a nice-looking piece of star anise to garnish

Put the ingredients into a mixing glass,
add plenty of cubed ice and stir gently
until the drink is very cold. Strain into a
chilled glass and add the garnish.

*Tastes a little strong, a little sour
and sweet*

Turn of the century
Cocktail

50 ml (1¾ fl oz) red vermouth
30 ml (1 fl oz) Canadian whisky
3 dashes of Boker's bitters
a twist of orange peel to garnish

Put the first two ingredients into a mixing
glass, add plenty of cubed ice and stir gently
until the drink is very cold. Strain into a chilled
glass and add the bitters and garnish.

Tastes strong and a little aromatic

Ali's barber

Cocktail

45 ml (1½ fl oz) Scotch whisky
15 ml (½ fl oz) Byrrh
15 ml (½ fl oz) Luxardo maraschino liqueur
15 ml (½ fl oz) fresh Meyer lemon
   juice (or fresh lemon juice)
a slice of Meyer lemon (or lemon) to garnish

Put the ingredients into a shaker, add
plenty of cubed ice and shake until
the shaker is very frosty. Strain into a
chilled glass and add the garnish.

*Tastes a little strong, sweet,
sour and aromatic*

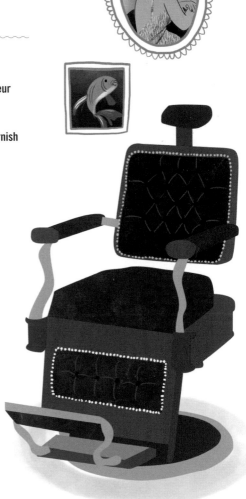

Swedish massage
Old-fashioned

45 ml (1½ fl oz) bourbon (or rye whiskey)
30 ml (1 fl oz) Swedish punsch
dash of orange bitters
brined olives or a twist of
   lemon peel to garnish

Put the ingredients into a mixing glass,
add plenty of cubed ice and stir gently
until the drink is very cold. Strain into a
chilled glass and add the garnish.

Tastes strong, sweet and a little aromatic

Boulevardiere
Champagne coupe

30 ml (1 fl oz) rye whiskey (or bourbon)
15 ml (½ fl oz) red vermouth
15 ml (½ fl oz) Campari
a brined olive such as Bella di
   Cerignola to garnish

Put the ingredients into a mixing glass,
add plenty of cubed ice and stir gently
until the drink is very cold. Strain into a
chilled glass and add the garnish.

Tastes strong, sweet and bitter

Swell hoofer
Cocktail

~~~~~~~~~~~~~~~~~~~~~~~~~~~~

30 ml (1 fl oz) Scotch whisky
30 ml (1 fl oz) Byrrh
½ teaspoon crème de Noyaux (or amaretto)
a maraschino cherry to garnish

Put the ingredients into a shaker, add
plenty of cubed ice and shake until the
shaker is very frosty. Fine-strain into a
chilled glass and add the garnish.

Tastes strong, sweet and aromatic

Tax evasion
Old-fashioned

~~~~~~~~~~~~~~~~~~~~~~~~~~~~

30 ml (1 fl oz) Scotch whisky
30 ml (1 fl oz) sloe gin
¼ teaspoon absinthe
dash of Angostura bitters
a twist of lemon peel to garnish

Put the ingredients into a glass, add
plenty of cubed ice and stir gently until
the drink is very cold. Add the garnish.

*Tastes strong, sweet, a little aromatic
and of aniseed*

The good times you never knew your grandma had

Champagne coupe

60 ml (2 fl oz) rye whiskey (preferably
  a good peppery one like Sazerac)
2 teaspoons crème de Noyaux (or amaretto)
1 teaspoon Kina l'Aero d'Or (or
  Cocchi Americano)
3 rose petals to garnish

Put the ingredients into a mixing glass, add
plenty of cubed ice and stir gently until the drink
is very cold. Strain into a chilled glass full of
fresh cubed ice and float the garnish on top.

Tastes strong, nutty and a little sweet

Bela Lugosi

Cocktail

45 ml (1½ fl oz) rye whiskey
  (preferably Sazerac rye)
30 ml (1 fl oz) Dubonnet
1½ teaspoons curaçao (or triple sec)
3 dashes of orange bitters
a twist of orange peel to garnish

Put the ingredients into a mixing glass,
add plenty of cubed ice and stir gently
until the drink is very cold. Strain into a
chilled glass and add the garnish.

*Tastes strong, sweet, aromatic
and a little bitter*

Sazerac

Old-fashioned

60 ml (2 fl oz) rye whiskey
  (preferably Sazerac rye)
1 teaspoon sugar syrup (see page 19)
dash of Peychaud's bitters
¼ teaspoon absinthe
a twist of orange peel to garnish

Put the first three ingredients into a mixing
glass, add plenty of cubed ice and stir
gently until the drink is very cold. Meanwhile,
put the absinthe into a chilled glass and
turn it gently to coat the inside. Strain
the contents of the mixing glass into the
prepared glass and add the garnish.

*Tastes strong, a little sweet,
aromatic and of aniseed*

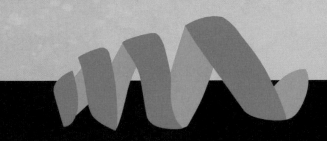

Mint julep

Julep cup or highball

8 mint leaves
2 teaspoons sugar syrup (see page 19)
60 ml (2 fl oz) rye whiskey (or bourbon)
2 drops of Angostura bitters
a mint sprig with a big piece of
   stalk still attached and a thin
   slice of orange to garnish

Put the first two ingredients into a mixing glass. Using the handle end of a wooden spoon, swirl the leaves around the glass (this will bruise them enough to extract the flavour but not so much as to make them taste like lawn clippings). Fill the serving glass to just over the top with crushed ice and tip this into the mixing glass along with the whiskey and bitters. Stir gently until the glass is frosty. Pour unstrained into the serving glass and stir gently until it is very frosty. Stick the mint stalk way down into the drink and float the orange slice on top.

Tastes strong, sweet and a little aromatic

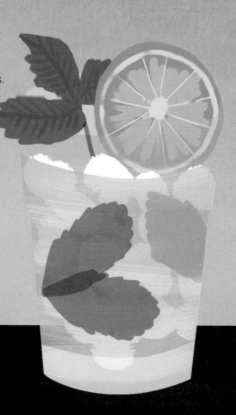

The sultan of swat
Cocktail

~~~~~~~~~~~~~~~~~~~~~~~~~~~~~~

30 ml (1 fl oz) Scotch whisky
15 ml (½ fl oz) Kina l'Aero d'Or
   (or Cocchi Americano)
a twist of orange peel to garnish

Put the ingredients into a mixing glass, add
plenty of cubed ice and stir gently until the
drink is very cold. Strain into a chilled glass
full of fresh cubed ice and add the garnish.

Tastes strong, a little sweet and bitter

Tight spot
Cocktail

~~~~~~~~~~~~~~~~~~~~~~~~~~~~~~

60 ml (2 fl oz) Canadian whisky
15 ml (½ fl oz) green chartreuse
1 teaspoon absinthe
a twist of orange peel to garnish

Put the ingredients into a shaker, add
plenty of cubed ice and shake until
the shaker is very frosty. Strain into a
chilled glass and add the garnish.

Tastes strong, sweet and of aniseed

Slippery Pete
Cocktail

60 ml (2 fl oz) rye whiskey
20 ml (¾ fl oz) Dubonnet
1 teaspoon sugar syrup (see page 19)
2 dashes of orange bitters
a maraschino cherry to garnish

Put the ingredients into a mixing glass,
add plenty of cubed ice and stir gently
until the drink is very cold. Strain into a
chilled glass and add the garnish.

Tastes strong, a little sweet and aromatic

Trouble in paradise
Cocktail

30 ml (1 fl oz) Canadian whisky
30 ml (1 fl oz) crème de Noyaux
  (or amaretto)
15 ml (½ fl oz) fresh lime juice
3 sugared almonds in a little
  fabric bag to garnish

Put the ingredients into a mixing glass, add plenty of cubed ice and stir gently until the drink is very cold. Strain into a chilled glass. Tie the garnish to the stem of the glass.

Tastes strong and a little aromatic

To the lost
Cocktail

60 ml (2 fl oz) Scotch whisky
2 teaspoons ginger syrup (see page 20)
dash of Peychaud's bitters
dash of Boker's bitters (or Angostura bitters)
a slice of orange to garnish

Put the first two ingredients into a mixing glass, add plenty of cubed ice and stir gently until the drink is very cold. Strain into a chilled glass and add the bitters and garnish.

Tastes strong and a little aromatic

TNT
Cocktail

30 ml (1 fl oz) Canadian whisky
30 ml (1 fl oz) absinthe
a nice-looking piece of star anise to garnish

Put the ingredients into a shaker, add
plenty of cubed ice and shake hard until
the shaker is very frosty. Fine-strain into
a chilled glass and add the garnish.

Tastes strong, sweet and of aniseed

Wet congress
Cocktail

60 ml (2 fl oz) bourbon
20 ml (¾ fl oz) crème de cacao
2 teaspoons green chartreuse
dash of Peychaud's bitters
a twist of orange peel to garnish

Put the ingredients into a mixing glass,
add plenty of cubed ice and stir gently
until the drink is very cold. Strain into a
chilled glass and add the garnish.

Tastes strong, a little sweet and aromatic

Orange satchmo
Old-fashioned

60 ml (2 fl oz) rye whiskey
2 teaspoons curaçao (or triple sec)
dash of Peychaud's bitters
¼ teaspoon absinthe
a twist of orange peel to garnish

Put the first three ingredients into a mixing
glass, add plenty of cubed ice and stir
gently until the drink is very cold. Meanwhile,
put the absinthe into a chilled glass and
turn it gently to coat the inside. Strain
the contents of the mixing glass into the
prepared glass and add the garnish.

*Tastes strong, a little sweet, a little
aromatic and of aniseed*

Emely's Manhattan

Cocktail or Old-fashioned

30 ml (1 fl oz) rye whiskey
30 ml (1 fl oz) cognac
30 ml (1 fl oz) Cocchi Vermouth di Torino
2 teaspoons liquid from a jar of
    jalapeño pickles
a maraschino cherry and a twist
    of orange peel to garnish

Put the ingredients into a mixing glass, add plenty of cubed ice and stir gently until the drink is very cold. Strain into a chilled glass (if using an old-fashioned glass add more cubed ice) and add the garnish.

Tastes strong, sweet, a little spicy and aromatic

Rye Manhattan

Cocktail or Old-fashioned

60 ml (2 fl oz) rye whiskey
15 ml (½ fl oz) red vermouth
dash of Angostura bitters
a twist of orange peel and a
    maraschino cherry to garnish

Put the ingredients into a mixing glass, add plenty of cubed ice and stir gently until the drink is very cold. Strain into a chilled glass (if using an old-fashioned glass add more cubed ice) and add the garnish.

Tastes strong, aromatic and a little sweet

Sidecar

American cocktail culture sweeps Europe

————————◄◼►————————

The temperance movement had some lovely ideas.
For example, one writer suggested that drunks could die from
'internal fires kindled often spontaneously from the fumes of alcohol'.

Another writer rather dramatically suggested that the
best punishment for people caught drinking was to
hang them from an aeroplane by the tongue.

The story of the *sidecar* itself is simple. It was either invented
in Paris or in London. It may or may not have been named for an
American army captain who would arrive at one of many bars via a
motorcycle sidecar. What is certain, however, is that it is delicious.

A COLLECTION OF BRANDY COCKTAILS

Sidecar
Cocktail

a slice of lemon and sugar for
   coating the rim of the glass
75 ml (2½ fl oz) cognac
20 ml (¾ fl oz) fresh lemon juice
15 ml (½ fl oz) curaçao (or triple sec)
a twist of lemon peel to garnish

First prepare a glass by rubbing the rim
with the slice of lemon so that the juice
covers about 1 cm (½ inch) of the outside
of the glass. Sprinkle sugar over the juice
while turning the glass so that a crust is
formed. Then put the ingredients into a
shaker, add plenty of cubed ice and shake
until the shaker is very frosty. Strain into
the prepared glass and add the garnish.

Tastes strong, a little sweet and sour

Génération perdue
Cocktail

~~~~~~~~~~~~~~~~~~~~~~~~~~

30 ml (1 fl oz) Dubonnet
15 ml (½ fl oz) cognac
15 ml (½ fl oz) Campari
a twist of orange peel and a maraschino
  cherry to garnish

Put the ingredients into a mixing glass, add
plenty of cubed ice and stir gently until the
drink is very cold. Strain into a chilled glass
full of fresh cubed ice and add the garnish.

Tastes strong, sweet and bitter

Between the sheets

Cocktail

20 ml (¾ fl oz) cognac
20 ml (¾ fl oz) white rum
20 ml (¾ fl oz) curaçao (or triple sec)
½ teaspoon fresh lemon juice
a twist of lemon peel to garnish

Put the ingredients into a mixing glass,
add plenty of cubed ice and stir gently
until the drink is very cold. Strain into
a chilled glass and add the garnish.

Tastes strong, a little sweet and sour

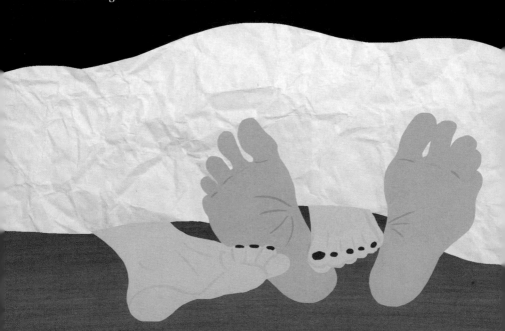

Brandy crusta
Wine goblet

a slice of lemon and sugar
  for coating the glass
the peel of a whole lemon
  or orange to garnish
60 ml (2 fl oz) cognac
1 teaspoon fresh lemon juice
½ teaspoon curaçao (or triple sec)
1 teaspoon sugar syrup (see page 19)
dash of Boker's bitters (or Angostura bitters)

Rub the slice of lemon liberally around one side of a glass then sprinkle sugar over the moistened glass so it forms a sugary crust — this is where the name comes from. Then take the peel and arrange it inside the glass so it spirals up to the top. Put the ingredients into a mixing glass, add plenty of cubed ice and stir gently until the drink is very cold. Strain into the prepared glass and add 1 cube of ice.

Tastes a little strong, sour, sweet and aromatic

Cognac Sazerac
Old-fashioned

60 ml (2 fl oz) cognac
1 teaspoon sugar syrup (see page 19)
dash of Peychaud's bitters
¼ teaspoon absinthe
a twist of orange peel to garnish

Put the first three ingredients into a mixing glass, add plenty of cubed ice and stir gently until the drink is very cold. Meanwhile, put the absinthe into a chilled glass and turn it gently to coat the inside. Strain the mix into the prepared glass and add the garnish.

Tastes strong, a little sweet, aromatic and of aniseed

Stinger
Cocktail

60 ml (2 fl oz) cognac
15 ml (½ fl oz) crème de menthe
  (either colour will do)
a mint sprig to garnish

Put the ingredients into a mixing glass,
add plenty of cubed ice and stir gently
until the drink is very cold. Strain into
a chilled glass and add the garnish.

Tastes strong, sweet and minty

Cake eater

Champagne coupe

〰〰〰〰〰〰〰〰〰〰〰

15 ml (½ fl oz) cognac
15 ml (½ fl oz) dark rum
15 ml (½ fl oz) crème de
 Noyaux (or amaretto)
15 ml (½ fl oz) apricot brandy
15 ml (½ fl oz) fresh lemon juice
 a twist of lemon peel to garnish

Put the ingredients into a shaker, add
plenty of cubed ice and shake hard
for 15 seconds. Fine-strain into a
chilled glass and add the garnish.

Tastes strong and aromatic

Cognac julep
Julep cup or Highball

8 mint leaves
2 teaspoons sugar syrup (see page 19)
60 ml (2 fl oz) cognac
a thin slice of orange, a thin slice of
   cucumber and a sprig of mint to garnish

Put the first two ingredients into a mixing
glass. Using the handle end of a wooden
spoon, swirl the leaves around the glass
(this will bruise them enough to extract the
flavour but not so much as to make them
taste like lawn clippings). Fill the serving
glass to just over the top with crushed ice
and tip this into the mixing glass along with
the cognac. Stir gently until the glass is
frosty. Pour unstrained into the serving glass
and stir gently until it is very frosty. Push the
cucumber and orange below the surface of
the drink and float the mint sprig on top.

Tastes strong, sweet and a little aromatic

Lindberg crossing
Old-fashioned

60 ml (2 fl oz) cognac
15 ml (½ fl oz) D.O.M. Benedictine
15 ml (½ fl oz) fresh lime juice
a slice of lime to garnish

Put the ingredients into a glass, add
plenty of cubed ice and stir gently until
the drink is very cold. Add the garnish.

Tastes strong, a little sweet and sour

Horsefeathers
Old-fashioned

30 ml (1 fl oz) cognac
30 ml (1 fl oz) dark rum
15 ml (½ fl oz) D.O.M. Benedictine
15 ml (½ fl oz) Luxardo maraschino liqueur
a twist of orange peel to garnish

Put the ingredients into a glass, add
plenty of cubed ice and stir gently until
the drink is very cold. Add the garnish.

Tastes strong, sweet and aromatic

Roffignac
Highball

45 ml (1½ fl oz) cognac
15 ml (½ fl oz) raspberry shrub (see page 21)
15 ml (½ fl oz) sugar syrup (see page 19)
approximately 90 ml (3 fl oz) soda water
  (club soda)
a twist of grapefruit peel to garnish

Put the first three ingredients into a glass,
add plenty of cubed ice and stir gently
until the drink is very cold. Top with soda
water, stir once and add the garnish.

Tastes sweet and a little sour

Vieux carré*
Old-fashioned

20 ml (¾ fl oz) cognac
20 ml (¾ fl oz) rye whiskey
20 ml (¾ fl oz) red vermouth
1 teaspoon D.O.M. Benedictine
2 dashes of Peychaud's bitters
2 dashes of Angostura bitters
a maraschino cherry to garnish

Put the ingredients into a mixing glass, add
plenty of cubed ice and stir gently until the
drink is very cold. Strain into a chilled glass
full of fresh cubed ice and add the garnish.

Tastes strong, sweet and aromatic

*This drink was actually invented just after the repeal
 of prohibition, but it is delicious.

Southside fizz

A gentleman, a murderer and a gin fizz

———————◀◻◎◻▶———————

Estimates place the income of Al Capone's organisation anywhere between $60 million and $108 million for the year 1927 alone.

Despite the fact that he bombed any bar that wouldn't buy his beer and routinely machine-gunned his enemies or beat them to death with baseball bats, he was well liked by ordinary people.

The Southside probably wasn't named after Chicago's South Side, nor drunk by Capone's gang. But its likely history of being named after a country club for rich *eggs* in Long Island just doesn't have the same gangster romance.

A COLLECTION OF COOLERS, RICKEYS AND FIZZES (OR TALL, REFRESHING DRINKS)

Southside fizz
Collins

60 ml (2 fl oz) dry gin
30 ml (1 fl oz) fresh lemon juice
15 ml (½ fl oz) sugar syrup (see page 19)
4 mint leaves
approximately 30 ml (1 fl oz) soda water
  (club soda)
a sprig of mint to garnish

Put the first four ingredients into a shaker,
add plenty of cubed ice and shake hard
until the shaker is very frosty. Strain into
a chilled glass filled with cubed ice, top
with soda water and add the garnish.

Tastes refreshing, a little sour and sweet

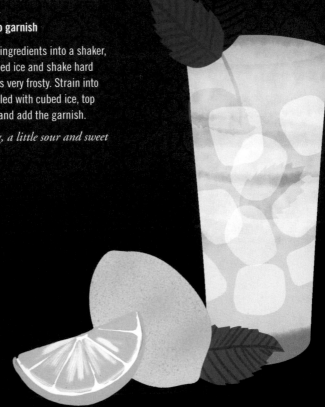

Cash or cheque?
Collins

45 ml (1½ fl oz) rye whiskey
15 ml (½ fl oz) homemade
  grenadine (see page 19)
1 teaspoon clove syrup (see page 20)
3 dashes of Peychaud's bitters
approximately 90 ml (3 fl oz) soda water
  (club soda)
a slice of orange to garnish

Put the first four ingredients into a shaker,
add plenty of cubed ice and shake hard
until the shaker is very frosty. Strain into
a chilled glass, add 1 cube of ice, top
with soda water and add the garnish.

Tastes refreshing, sweet and aromatic

Byrrh cassis
Collins

30 ml (1 fl oz) Byrrh
15 ml (½ fl oz) crème de cassis
approximately 100 ml (3½ fl oz) soda water
  (club soda)
a twist of lemon peel to garnish

Put the first two ingredients into a mixing
glass, add plenty of cubed ice and stir
gently until the drink is very cold. Strain
into a chilled glass, add 1 cube of ice and
top with soda water. Add the garnish.

Tastes strong and a little aromatic

Cognac cooler
Highball

45 ml (1½ fl oz) cognac
15 ml (½ fl oz) port (or muscat)
1 teaspoon crème de cassis
2 dashes of Peychaud's bitters
approximately 90 ml (3 fl oz) soda water
  (club soda)
a slice of lemon to garnish

Put the first four ingredients into a
glass, add plenty of cubed ice and stir
until the glass is frosty. Top with soda
water, stir once and add the garnish.

Tastes refreshing and a little sweet

Cora's cooler
Collins

100 ml (3½ fl oz) dry riesling
2 teaspoons cognac
2 teaspoons Luxardo maraschino liqueur
2 teaspoons sugar syrup (see page 19)
approximately 60 ml (2 fl oz) soda water
  (club soda)
a slice of lemon to garnish

Put the first four ingredients into a mixing
glass, add plenty of cubed ice and stir gently
until the drink is very cold. Strain into a chilled
glass, top with soda water and add the garnish.

Tastes refreshing, a little sweet and sour

Claret cooler
Highball

150 ml (5 fl oz) red wine*
15 ml (½ fl oz) cognac
25 ml (¾ fl oz) Luxardo maraschino liqueur
1 teaspoon fresh lemon juice
approximately 60 ml (2 fl oz) soda water
   (club soda)
a slice of lemon to garnish

Put the first four ingredients into a glass,
add plenty of cubed ice and stir gently
until the drink is very cold. Top with soda
water, stir once and add the garnish.

Tastes refreshing and a little sweet

*This is a good way to use wine
that is getting past its best.

Highland cooler
Collins

45 ml (1½ fl oz) Scotch whisky
15 ml (½ fl oz) fresh lemon juice
1 teaspoon sugar syrup (see page 19)
2 dashes of Angostura bitters
approximately 90 ml (3 fl oz) soda water
   (club soda)
a slice of lemon to garnish

Put the first four ingredients into a mixing
glass, add plenty of cubed ice and stir gently
until the drink is very cold. Strain into a chilled
glass, top with soda water and add the garnish.

Tastes refreshing, a little sour and aromatic

'Fishing' trip
Cocktail

30 ml (1 fl oz) bourbon
30 ml (1 fl oz) Swedish punsch
30 ml (1 fl oz) fresh orange juice
approximately 100 ml (3½ fl oz) soda water
   (club soda)
a slice of orange to garnish

Put the first three ingredients into a mixing
glass, add plenty of cubed ice and stir gently
until the drink is very cold. Strain into a chilled
glass full of fresh cubed ice, top with soda
water and add the garnish.

*Tastes sweet, refreshing and
a little aromatic*

Dubonnet citron

Highball

40 ml (1¼ fl oz) Dubonnet
2 teaspoons fresh lemon juice
2 teaspoons sugar syrup (see page 19)
approximately 100 ml (3½ fl oz) soda water
  (club soda)
a slice of lemon to garnish

Put the first three ingredients into a mixing glass, add plenty of cubed ice and stir gently until the drink is very cold. Strain into a chilled glass full of fresh cubed ice, top with soda water and float the garnish on top.

Tastes refreshing, sweet, a little sour and aromatic

Gin rickey

Highball

45 ml (1½ fl oz) dry gin
¼ medium-sized lime
approximately 120 ml (4 fl oz) soda water
  (club soda)

Fill a glass with cubed ice, pour in the gin, squeeze the lime on top and drop the squeezed lime shell into the glass. Top with soda water.

Tastes refreshing and a little sour

Tom Collins
Collins

60 ml (2 fl oz) Old Tom gin (or dry gin)
30 ml (1 fl oz) fresh lemon juice
15 ml (½ fl oz) sugar syrup (see page 19)
approximately 90 ml (3 fl oz) soda water
  (club soda)
a slice of lime to garnish

Put the first three ingredients into a mixing
glass, add plenty of cubed ice and stir
gently until the drink is very cold. Pour into
a glass filled with fresh cubed ice, top
with soda water and add the garnish.

*Tastes refreshing, strong, sour and
a little sweet*

Giggle water

Collins

~~~~~~~~~~~~~~~~~~~~~~~~~~~~~~~~~~~

30 ml (1 fl oz) Campari
30 ml (1 fl oz) raspberry shrub (see page 21)
approximately 90 ml (3 fl oz) Brut
  Champagne (or dry sparkling wine)
a twist of grapefruit peel to garnish

Put the first two ingredients into a
shaker, add plenty of cubed ice and shake
hard until the shaker is very frosty. Fill
a glass halfway with crushed ice and
fine-strain the drink into it. Top with
Champagne and float the garnish on top.

Tastes refreshing, bitter, sweet
and a little sour

Puttin' on the spritz
Highball

45 ml (1½ fl oz) Dubonnet
30 ml (1 fl oz) blueberry shrub (see page 21)
15 ml (½ fl oz) Old Tom gin (or dry gin)
approximately 90 ml (3 fl oz) soda water
  (club soda)
5 fresh blueberries to garnish

Put the first three ingredients into a
glass, add plenty of cubed ice and stir
until the glass is frosty. Top with soda
water, stir once and add the garnish.

Tastes refreshing, a little sour and sweet

Gimlet
Old-fashioned

60 ml (2 fl oz) Old Tom gin (or dry gin)
30 ml (1 fl oz) sugar syrup (see page 19)
30 ml (1 fl oz) fresh lime juice
60 ml (2 fl oz) still water
a twist of lime peel to garnish

Fill a glass with cubed ice, add all ingredients
in order and stir gently until it is very cold. Add
the garnish.

Tastes sweet, sour and weirdly cooling

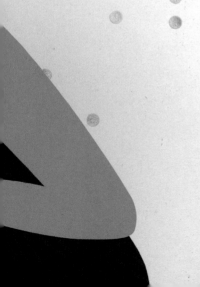

Kingston cooler
Highball

30 ml (1 fl oz) dark rum
15 ml (½ fl oz) dry vermouth
15 ml (½ fl oz) cherry brandy (or Guignolet)
2 teaspoons fresh lime juice
approximately 150 ml (5 fl oz) soda water
 (club soda)
a slice of lime to garnish

Put the first four ingredients into a shaker,
add plenty of cubed ice and shake hard
until the shaker is very frosty. Strain into
a chilled glass, add 1 cube of ice, top
with soda water and add the garnish.

Tastes refreshing, a little sour and sweet

Gin fizz
Old-fashioned

60 ml (2 fl oz) dry gin
30 ml (1 fl oz) fresh lemon juice
15 ml (½ fl oz) sugar syrup (see page 19)
approximately 20 ml (¾ fl oz) soda water
 (club soda)
a slice of lemon to garnish

Put the first three ingredients into a shaker,
add plenty of cubed ice and shake hard
until the shaker is very frosty. Strain into
a chilled glass filled with cubed ice, top
with soda water and add the garnish.

Tastes refreshing, a little sour and sweet

Applesauce!
Old-fashioned

30 ml (1 fl oz) Plymouth gin
60 ml (2 fl oz) good-quality applesauce
1 teaspoon sugar syrup (see page 19)
1 teaspoon fresh lemon juice
a candied cherry, a slice of smoked
  kransky or chorizo and a slice of
  apple on a skewer to garnish

Put the ingredients into a shaker, add
an old-fashioned glass full of crushed
ice and shake until the applesauce is
thoroughly incorporated. Pour unstrained
into the glass and add the garnish.

Tastes sweet, a little sour and savoury

PLYMOUTH
GIN

Pink gin*
Cocktail

60 ml (2 fl oz) Old Tom gin (or dry gin)
30 ml (1 fl oz) still water
exactly 2 drops of Angostura bitters
a twist of lemon peel to garnish

Put the ingredients into a glass, add
1 cube of ice and stir gently until the
drink is cold. Add the garnish.

Tastes strong and a little aromatic

*An old sailor's drink and my late grandmother's
favourite. The specific proportions are essential.

Silver fizz
Collins

60 ml (2 fl oz) dry gin
30 ml (1 fl oz) fresh lemon juice
15 ml (½ fl oz) sugar syrup (see page 19)
1 egg white
approximately 20 ml (¾ fl oz) soda water
  (club soda)
a slice of lemon to garnish

Put the first four ingredients into a shaker,
add plenty of cubed ice and shake hard
until the shaker is very frosty. Strain
into a chilled glass filled with cubed ice,
top with soda and add the garnish.

*Tastes refreshing, a little creamy, sour
and sweet*

The yellow roller
Collins

45 ml (1½ fl oz) Canadian whisky
15 ml (½ fl oz) crème de pamplemousse rosé
¼ medium-sized lemon
approximately 90 ml (3 fl oz) soda water
  (club soda)

Put the first two ingredients into a glass, add
plenty of cubed ice then squeeze the lemon into
the glass and drop it in as a garnish. Top with
soda and stir briefly to incorporate.

Tastes refreshing and a little fruity

Singapore sling*
Collins

30 ml (1 fl oz) dry gin
30 ml (1 fl oz) cherry brandy (or Guignolet)
30 ml (1 fl oz) D.O.M. Benedictine
30 ml (1 fl oz) fresh lime juice
dash of Angostura bitters
approximately 60 ml (2 fl oz) soda water
  (club soda)
a twist of lime peel and a
  maraschino cherry to garnish

Put the first five ingredients into a shaker, add plenty of cubed ice and shake until the shaker is very frosty. Strain into a chilled glass full of cubed ice, top with soda water and add the garnish.

Tastes refreshing, sweet and a little sour

*This recipe is adapted from one written on a scrap of paper by a Raffles Hotel customer in Singapore in the 1930s.

That's the berries
Highball

30 ml (1 fl oz) Campari
30 ml (1 fl oz) strawberry shrub (see page 21)
approximately 90 ml (3 fl oz) soda water
  (club soda)
a twist of orange peel to garnish

Put the first two ingredients into a glass, add plenty of cubed ice and stir until the glass is frosty. Top with soda water, stir once and add the garnish.

Tastes refreshing, bitter and sweet

Egyptian princess
Old-fashioned

45 ml (1½ fl oz) Canadian whisky
30 ml (1 fl oz) raspberry shrub (see page 21)
dash of Angostura bitters
approximately 90 ml (3 fl oz) soda water
  (club soda)
a slice of lime to garnish

Put the first three ingredients into a
glass, add plenty of cubed ice and stir
gently until the drink is very cold. Top
with soda water and add the garnish.

Tastes sweet and a little sour

C-A-P-O-N-E kapow!
Collins

60 ml (2 fl oz) dry gin
20 ml (¾ fl oz) kiwi syrup (see page 20)
30 ml (1 fl oz) fresh lemon juice
4 mint leaves
approximately 90 ml (3 fl oz) soda water
  (club soda)
a slice of kiwi fruit with a mint
  sprig stuck in it to garnish

Put the first four ingredients into a shaker,
add plenty of cubed ice and shake hard
until the shaker is very frosty. Strain into
a chilled glass filled with cubed ice, top
with soda water and add the garnish.

Tastes refreshing, a little sour and sweet

Sheik
Highball

60 ml (2 fl oz) dry gin
30 ml (1 fl oz) raspberry shrub (see page 21)
approximately 90 ml (3 fl oz) soda water
  (club soda)
a slice of lemon to garnish

Put the first two ingredients into a
glass, add plenty of cubed ice and stir
gently until the drink is very cold. Top
with soda water and add the garnish.

Tastes refreshing, a little sweet and sour

Frosted Phyllis
Collins

30 ml (1 fl oz) Old Tom gin
15 ml (½ fl oz) blueberry shrub (see page 21)
approximately 100 ml (3½ fl oz) soda water
  (club soda)
a slice of lime to garnish

Fill a glass with cubed ice, add the
ingredients in order and stir. Float the
slice of lime on top of the drink.

Tastes refreshing, a little sweet and sour

Picador

*Mexico, tequila and the
sour legacy of prohibition*

———◦■◦———

Crime rates soared in the States during prohibition and gave
rise to opportunists. Mexico's Gulf Cartel got its start during
this time when its founder Juan Guerra started smuggling
whisky, rum and tequila across the Texas border.

However, according to the 1920 Anti Saloon League yearbook,
some towns were so convinced that crime would disappear
with prohibition that they actually sold their jails.

While prohibition gave tequila a boost in popularity in
America, the English were the first to apply it to cocktails. The
picador, invented in London around the end of prohibition,
bears a remarkable similarity to a margarita without the
salt rim, though it predates it by at least ten years.

A COLLECTION OF TEQUILA-BASED COCKTAILS

Picador*
Cocktail

30 ml (1 fl oz) tequila blanco
15 ml (½ fl oz) curaçao (or triple sec)
15 ml (½ fl oz) fresh lime juice
a slice of lime to garnish

Put the ingredients into a shaker, add
plenty of cubed ice and shake hard until
the shaker is very frosty. Fine-strain into
a chilled glass and add the garnish.

Tastes a little strong, sweet and sour

*This 1930s cocktail bears a striking
resemblance to a certain modern one. Feel
free to modernise it with a salt rim!

Matador

Champagne coupe

30 ml (1 fl oz) tequila blanco
30 ml (1 fl oz) dry vermouth
30 ml (1 fl oz) curaçao (or triple sec)
a twist of orange peel to garnish

Put the ingredients into a mixing glass,
add plenty of cubed ice and stir gently
until the drink is very cold. Strain into
a chilled glass and add the garnish.

Tastes strong, sweet and aromatic

Everything's Jake
in paradise

Cocktail

30 ml (1 fl oz) tequila blanco
60 ml (2 fl oz) Swedish punsch
a small wedge of pineapple with
   the skin on to garnish

Put the ingredients into a mixing glass,
add plenty of cubed ice and stir gently until
the drink is very cold. Strain into a chilled
glass, then cut a slice into the wedge of
pineapple and fix it to the rim of the glass.

Tastes strong and a little aromatic

Earth and heaven
Cocktail

45 ml (1½ fl oz) tequila blanco
30 ml (1 fl oz) D.O.M. Benedictine
1 teaspoon dry vermouth
a maraschino cherry to garnish

Put the ingredients into a mixing glass, add
plenty of cubed ice and stir gently until the
drink is very cold. Strain into a chilled glass
and add the garnish.

Tastes strong, sweet and a little aromatic

Fast times in Matamoros

Champagne coupe

〜〜〜〜〜〜〜〜〜〜

30 ml (1 fl oz) tequila blanco
15 ml (½ fl oz) Byrrh
15 ml (½ fl oz) Dubonnet
1 teaspoon homemade
  grenadine (see page 19)
a twist of lemon peel to garnish

Put the ingredients into a mixing glass,
add plenty of cubed ice and stir gently
until the drink is very cold. Strain into
a chilled glass and add the garnish.

Tastes strong, sweet and aromatic

Slumming with a debutante

Cocktail

〜〜〜〜〜〜〜〜〜〜

45 ml (1½ fl oz) tequila blanco
45 ml (1½ fl oz) Kina l'Aero d'Or
  (or Cocchi Americano)
15 ml (½ fl oz) crème de cacao
2 dashes of orange bitters
a twist of orange peel to garnish

Put the ingredients into a mixing glass,
add plenty of cubed ice and stir gently
until the drink is very cold. Strain into
a chilled glass and add the garnish.

Tastes strong, sweet and a little bitter

Creole fashioned

Cocktail

30 ml (1 fl oz) tequila blanco
15 ml (½ fl oz) dark rum
15 ml (½ fl oz) Swedish punsch
15 ml (½ fl oz) curaçao (or triple sec)
2 dashes of Peychaud's bitters
a twist of orange peel to garnish

Put the ingredients into a mixing glass, add plenty of cubed ice and stir gently until the drink is very cold. Strain into a chilled glass full of fresh cubed ice and add the garnish.

Tastes strong, sweet and aromatic

Toreador

Cocktail

60 ml (2 fl oz) tequila blanco
20 ml (¾ fl oz) fresh lime juice
15 ml (½ fl oz) apricot brandy
a slice of lime to garnish

Put the ingredients into a shaker, add
plenty of cubed ice and shake hard until
the shaker is very frosty. Fine-strain into
a chilled glass and add the garnish.

Tastes a little strong, sweet and sour

Clover club

A flagrant, pink and fluffy disregard
for the established social order

'*You know we're charging $30 a quart for Champagne and you know it*
isn't Champagne. Tell your young lady to take gin and like it.'
Texas Guinan

Ladies of the 1920s were not only free to go to speakeasies, they
also ran several of them. The most famous was the silent film
actress 'Texas' Guinan, whose 300 Club played host to the most
famous actors and the most powerful elite members of society.
She famously greeted all her guests with, 'Hello, suckers!'

The *clover club*, always a hit with the dames, was
one of the most popular cocktails of the day.

A COLLECTION OF DRINKS MADE WITH SOMETHING
SWEET, SOMETHING SOUR AND SOMETHING GIN

Clover club
Champagne coupe

45 ml (1½ fl oz) dry gin
20 ml (¾ fl oz) fresh lemon juice
15 ml (½ fl oz) raspberry shrub (see page 21)
  (or homemade grenadine, see page 19)
1 teaspoon dry vermouth
1 egg white
a maraschino cherry to garnish

Put the ingredients into a shaker, add
plenty of cubed ice and shake very hard
for 30 seconds. Fine-strain into a chilled
glass and float the cherry on top.

Tastes sweet, a little sour and creamy

Bee's knees
Cocktail

honey
80 ml (2½ fl oz) dry gin
20 ml (¾ fl oz) honey syrup (see page 20)
20 ml (¾ fl oz) fresh lemon juice

Prepare a glass by drizzling the honey around the inside of the glass. Put the rest of the ingredients into a mixing glass, add plenty of cubed ice and stir gently until the drink is very cold. Strain into the prepared glass.

Tastes strong, sweet, and sour

The last word
Cocktail

20 ml (¾ fl oz) dry gin
20 ml (¾ fl oz) green chartreuse
20 ml (¾ fl oz) Luxardo maraschino liqueur
20 ml (¾ fl oz) fresh lime juice
a slice of lime to garnish

Put the ingredients into a shaker, add plenty of cubed ice and shake hard until the shaker is very frosty. Strain into a chilled glass and add the garnish.

Tastes strong, tart, herbal and sweet

Something gorgeous*
Cocktail

30 ml (1 fl oz) dry gin
15 ml (½ fl oz) Kina l'Aero d'Or
   (or Cocchi Americano)
15 ml (½ fl oz) elderflower cordial
15 ml (½ fl oz) fresh lime juice
a peeled rambutan or lychee to garnish

Put the ingredients into a shaker, add
plenty of cubed ice and shake until
the shaker is very frosty. Strain into a
chilled glass and add the garnish.

Tastes sour, a little sweet and strong

* *'If personality is an unbroken series of successful
gestures, then there was something gorgeous about
him, some heightened sensitivity to the promises
of life.'* – F. Scott Fitzgerald, The Great Gatsby.

With short skirts and shorter hair
Old-fashioned

40 ml (1¼ fl oz) dry gin
20 ml (¾ fl oz) fresh orange juice
1 teaspoon curaçao (or triple sec)
1 teaspoon ginger syrup (see page 20)
a slice of ginger and a twist of
   orange peel to garnish

Put the ingredients into a mixing glass, add
plenty of cubed ice and stir gently until
the drink is very cold. Pour unstrained
into a glass and add the garnish.

*Tastes a little sweet, a little sour
and aromatic*

Aviation
Cocktail

45 ml (1½ fl oz) Plymouth gin
20 ml (¾ fl oz) fresh lemon juice
1 teaspoon crème de violette
1 teaspoon Luxardo maraschino liqueur
a maraschino cherry to garnish

Put the ingredients into a mixing glass,
add plenty of cubed ice and stir gently
until the drink is very cold. Strain into
a chilled glass and add the garnish.

Tastes a little sweet, sour and aromatic

Bronx I
Cocktail

60 ml (2 fl oz) dry gin
15 ml (½ fl oz) red vermouth
1 teaspoon dry vermouth
15 ml (½ fl oz) fresh orange juice
a twist of orange peel to garnish

Put the ingredients into a mixing glass,
add plenty of cubed ice and stir gently
until the drink is very cold. Strain into
a chilled glass and add the garnish.

Tastes strong and a little sweet

Bronx II
Cocktail

30 ml (1 fl oz) dry gin
30 ml (1 fl oz) dry vermouth
30 ml (1 fl oz) red vermouth
30 ml (1 fl oz) fresh orange juice
dash of orange bitters
a twist of orange peel to garnish

Put the ingredients into a mixing glass,
add plenty of cubed ice and stir gently
until the drink is very cold. Strain into
a chilled glass and add the garnish.

Tastes sweet, a little sour and strong

Bronx cheer

Champagne coupe

40 ml (1¼ fl oz) dry gin
20 ml (¾ fl oz) Byrrh
2 teaspoons curaçao (or triple sec)
2 teaspoons fresh orange juice
dash of orange bitters
a slice of orange to garnish

Put the ingredients into a mixing glass,
add plenty of cubed ice and stir gently
until the drink is very cold. Strain into
a chilled glass and add the garnish.

Tastes strong, bitter and sweet

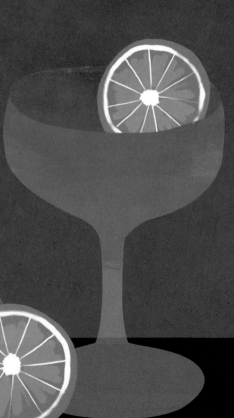

Corpse reviver No. 2
Cocktail

~~~~~~~~~~~~~~~~~~~~~~~~~~~~~~~~~~~

30 ml (1 fl oz) dry gin
30 ml (1 fl oz) Kina l'Aero d'Or
   (or Cocchi Americano)
30 ml (1 fl oz) curaçao (or triple sec)
30 ml (1 fl oz) fresh lemon juice
¼ teaspoon absinthe
a twist of lemon peel to garnish

Put the ingredients into a shaker, add
plenty of cubed ice and shake until
the shaker is very frosty. Strain into a
chilled glass and add the garnish.

Tastes sweet, a little bitter,
sour and aromatic

Her voice was full of money

Champagne coupe

45 ml (1½ fl oz) Plymouth gin (or dry gin)
15 ml (½ fl oz) raspberry liqueur
    (preferably French)
15 ml (½ fl oz) fresh lemon juice
1 teaspoon dry vermouth
1 teaspoon sugar syrup (see page 19)
1 egg white
a few fresh raspberries to garnish

Put the ingredients into a shaker, add
plenty of cubed ice and shake very hard
for 30 seconds. Fine-strain into a chilled
glass and float the raspberries on top.

*Tastes strong, sweet, sour, creamy and
has a delightful hint of the aromatic*

Hotsy-totsy

Wine goblet

60 ml (2 fl oz) dry gin
60 ml (2 fl oz) fresh orange juice
15 ml (½ fl oz) apricot brandy
1 teaspoon clove syrup (see page 20)
a good-looking star anise and a
    twist of orange peel to garnish

Put the ingredients into a mixing glass,
add plenty of cubed ice and stir gently
until the drink is very cold. Strain into
a chilled glass and add the garnish.

*Tastes orangey, a little sweet,
sour and aromatic*

Gin daisy
Champagne coupe

~~~~~~~~~~~~~~~~~~~~~~~

60 ml (2 fl oz) dry gin
15 ml (½ fl oz) fresh lemon juice
15 ml (½ fl oz) homemade
   grenadine (see page 19)
a maraschino cherry to garnish

Put the ingredients into a shaker, add
plenty of cubed ice and shake hard
until the drink is very cold. Fine-strain
into a glass and add the garnish.

Tastes a little strong, sour and sweet.

Petting pantry
Cocktail

~~~~~~~~~~~~~~~~~~~~~~~

60 ml (2 fl oz) dry gin
25 ml (¾ fl oz) passionfruit pulp
   from 1 medium-sized fruit
2 teaspoons sugar syrup (see page 19)
1 teaspoon orange curaçao (or triple sec)
1 egg white

Put the ingredients into a shaker, add
plenty of cubed ice and shake very hard for
30 seconds. Strain through a hawthorne
strainer* into a chilled glass so that the
passionfruit seeds end up in the glass.

*Tastes a little strong, sweet,
sour and creamy*

*A hawthorne strainer is a flat metal strainer with
 a wire coil around the edge that fits into a cocktail
 shaker. It will strain out the big bits of ice, but
 will allow the passionfruit seeds to go through.

Moonlight caper
Cocktail

~~~~~~~~~~~~~~~~~~~~~~~~~

45 ml (1½ fl oz) yellow gin (or dry gin)
20 ml (¾ fl oz) fresh lime juice
2 teaspoons curaçao (or triple sec)
1 teaspoon crème de violette
a twist of orange peel to garnish

Put the ingredients into a mixing glass,
add plenty of cubed ice and stir gently
until the drink is very cold. Strain into
a chilled glass and add the garnish.

Tastes strong, a little sweet and sour

Plum delicious
Cocktail

~~~~~~~~~~~~~~~~~~~~~~~~~

30 ml (1 fl oz) sloe gin
20 ml (¾ fl oz) Old Tom gin
20 ml (¾ fl oz) Byrrh
2 teaspoons fresh lemon juice
a maraschino cherry to garnish

Put the ingredients into a mixing glass,
add plenty of cubed ice and stir gently
until the drink is very cold. Strain into
a chilled glass and add the garnish.

Tastes a little strong, sweet and sour

Jockey club
Cocktail

60 ml (2 fl oz) dry gin
1 teaspoon fresh lemon juice
1 teaspoon crème de Noyaux (or amaretto)
dash of Angostura bitters
dash of orange bitters
a twist of lemon peel to garnish

Put the ingredients into a shaker, add
plenty of cubed ice and shake hard until
the shaker is very frosty. Fine-strain into
a chilled glass and add the garnish.

Tastes strong, a little sour and aromatic

White lady
Cocktail

60 ml (2 fl oz) dry gin
20 ml (¾ fl oz) fresh lemon juice
2–4 teaspoons curaçao (or triple sec)
1 egg white
a thin slice of lemon to garnish

Put the ingredients into a shaker, shake
hard without ice for 20 seconds, then add
plenty of cubed ice and shake hard for another
10 seconds. Fine-strain into a chilled glass and
float the lemon carefully on top of the foam.

*Tastes a little creamy, strong, sour and,
if you use 4 teaspoons of liqueur, sweet*

Ramos gin fizz

New Orleans — the city that forgot prohibition existed

⬤■⬤

During 1923 a prohibition agent, delightfully named Izzy Einstein, timed how long it took him to buy illegal hooch from the time he got off the train in several major cities. The winner hands down was New Orleans at 35 seconds.

With a major seaport providing almost unlimited access to the vast booze caches of the Caribbean and Mexico, New Orleans never paid much attention to prohibition. They didn't have blind pigs and speakeasies, just restaurants and bars.

The *ramos gin fizz*, along with the *sazerac* and the *absinthe frappé* were the most famous New Orleans drinks of the day.

A COLLECTION OF DRINKS WITH MILK AND CREAM

Ramos gin fizz

Collins

60 ml (2 fl oz) dry gin
15 ml (½ fl oz) fresh lemon juice
15 ml (½ fl oz) fresh lime juice
30 ml (1 fl oz) sugar syrup (see page 19)
30 ml (1 fl oz) pouring cream
1 egg white
4 drops of orange blossom water
approximately 30 ml (1 fl oz) soda water
   (club soda)

Put the first seven ingredients into a shaker,
add plenty of cubed ice and shake hard for
2 full minutes. Strain into a glass, add the
soda water and swish once to incorporate.

*Tastes creamy, a little sweet, sour
and aromatic*

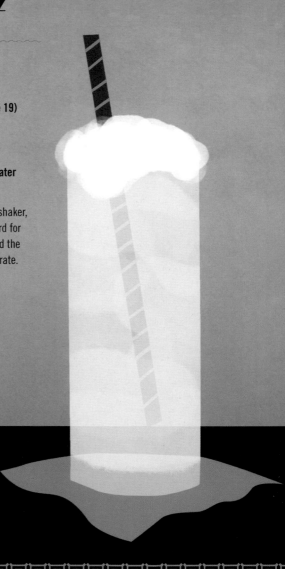

35 second fizz

Collins

30 ml (1 fl oz) Old Tom gin
45 ml (1½ fl oz) crème de
  Noyaux (or amaretto)
½ teaspoon sugar syrup (see page 19)
15 ml (½ fl oz) fresh lime juice
15 ml (½ fl oz) fresh lemon juice
30 ml (1 fl oz) pouring cream
1 egg white
approximately 30 ml (1 fl oz) soda water
  (club soda)

Put the first seven ingredients into a
shaker, shake hard for 1 minute, then
add cubed ice to the shaker and shake
for a further minute. Strain into a chilled
glass, top with soda and give it a single
thorough but brief stir to incorporate.

Tastes creamy, a little sour and sweet

Ichbien

Cocktail

45 ml (1½ fl oz) cognac
15 ml (½ fl oz) curaçao (or triple sec)
1 teaspoon sugar syrup (see page 19)
60 ml (2 fl oz) milk
1 egg yolk
freshly grated nutmeg to garnish

Put the ingredients into a shaker, add plenty
of cubed ice and shake until the shaker is very
frosty. Strain into a chilled glass and sprinkle
a little nutmeg over the top of the drink.

Tastes sweet, creamy and a little aromatic

Brandy Alexander
Champagne coupe

30 ml (1 fl oz) cognac
30 ml (1 fl oz) crème de cacao
30 ml (1 fl oz) pouring cream

Put the ingredients into a shaker, add plenty of cubed ice and shake hard until the shaker is very frosty. Fine-strain into a chilled glass.

Tastes sweet and creamy

Sheba sheba
Cocktail

60 ml (2 fl oz) dry gin
30 ml (1 fl oz) fresh lemon juice
30 ml (1 fl oz) homemade
  grenadine (see page 19)
1 teaspoon sugar syrup (see page 19)
½ teaspoon rosewater
30 ml (1 fl oz) pouring cream
1 egg white
approximately 30 ml (1 fl oz) soda water
  (club soda)

Put the first seven ingredients into a shaker, add plenty of cubed ice and shake hard for 2 full minutes. Strain into a glass, add the soda and swish once to incorporate.

Tastes creamy, a little sweet, sour and aromatic

Alexander cocktail

Champagne coupe

30 ml (1 fl oz) dry gin
30 ml (1 fl oz) crème de cacao
15 ml (½ fl oz) pouring cream

Put the ingredients into a shaker, add plenty of cubed ice and shake hard until the shaker is very frosty. Fine-strain into a chilled glass.

Tastes sweet and creamy

Whizz-doodle

Champagne coupe

20 ml (¾ fl oz) dry gin
20 ml (¾ fl oz) Scotch whisky
20 ml (¾ fl oz) crème de cacao
20 ml (¾ fl oz) pouring cream

Put the ingredients into a shaker, add plenty of cubed ice and shake hard until the shaker is very frosty. Fine-strain into a chilled glass.

Tastes sweet and creamy

Mont Blanc
Cocktail

45 ml (1½ fl oz) cognac
30 ml (1 fl oz) unsweetened chestnut puree
30 ml (1 fl oz) sugar syrup (see page 19)
30 ml (1 fl oz) pouring cream
1 teaspoon crème de Noyaux (or amaretto)
freshly grated nutmeg to garnish

Put the ingredients into a shaker, add plenty of cubed ice and shake hard until the shaker is very frosty. Fine-strain into a chilled glass and sprinkle the nutmeg on top.

Tastes sweet and creamy

Gin and milk
Highball

60 ml (2 fl oz) Old Tom gin
90 ml (3 fl oz) milk

Half fill a glass with cubed ice, add the ingredients and stir.

Tastes unsurprisingly milky and very surprisingly not horrible

Bank's closed

Miscellany

Prohibition worked so well that New York City is estimated to have had over 30,000 speakeasies, some of which are still open as clubs today.

The 1920s also saw the invention of the 'booze cruise', where boats would head into international waters and do circles while the passengers got spifflicated. This idea of a boat ride to nowhere caught on and became the foundation for today's cruise industry.

Alcohol was never completely outlawed during prohibition: it could be prescribed by physicians. After Winston Churchill was hit by a car in New York City in 1931, the attending doctor prescribed him a minimum of 250 ml (8½ fl oz) of spirits per day!

DRINKS THAT SIMPLY WEREN'T WELCOME IN THE OTHER CHAPTERS

Chocolate cocktail I

Cocktail

~~~~~~~~~~~~~~~~~~~~~~

30 ml (1 fl oz) Luxardo maraschino liqueur
30 ml (1 fl oz) yellow chartreuse
1 teaspoon Dutch (unsweetened)
    cocoa powder
1 whole egg

Put the ingredients into a shaker, add plenty
of cubed ice and shake hard until the shaker
is very frosty. Fine-strain into a chilled glass.

Tastes strong, sweet and chocolatey

Chocolate cocktail II
Cocktail

45 ml (1½ fl oz) D.O.M. Benedictine
20 ml (¾ fl oz) rye whiskey
1 teaspoon Dutch (unsweetened)
　cocoa powder
1 whole egg

Put the ingredients into a shaker, add plenty
of cubed ice and shake hard until the shaker
is very frosty. Fine-strain into a chilled glass.

Tastes strong, sweet and chocolatey

The beeswax
Old-fashioned

30 ml (1 fl oz) absinthe
30 ml (1 fl oz) crème de menthe
a mint sprig to garnish

Put the ingredients into a mixing glass, add
plenty of cubed ice and stir gently until the
drink is very cold. Strain into a chilled glass
full of fresh cubed ice and add the garnish.

Tastes strong, sweet, of aniseed and mint

Nineteen twenty cocktail

Champagne coupe

30 ml (1 fl oz) dry vermouth
15 ml (½ fl oz) kirsch
15 ml (½ fl oz) dry gin
1 teaspoon redcurrant syrup (see page 20)
   (or homemade grenadine, see page 19)
½ teaspoon absinthe
a twist of grapefruit peel to garnish

Put the ingredients into a shaker, add plenty of cubed ice and shake hard until the shaker is very frosty. Fine-strain into a chilled glass.

Tastes a little strong, sweet and strangely like a feijoa

Flip's absence

Large milkshake glass

30 ml (1 fl oz) Old Tom gin
30 ml (1 fl oz) absinthe
15 ml (½ fl oz) sugar syrup (see page 19)
250 ml (8½ fl oz) chilled milk
pinch of freshly grated nutmeg to garnish

Put the ingredients into a cream whipper, charge with N$_2$O. Shake it until the contents become obviously frothy then invert and discharge the contents into a glass. Sprinkle the nutmeg over the drink.

Tastes sweet, milky and a little of aniseed

Swiss
Cocktail

~~~~~~~~~~~~~~~~~~~~~~~~~~~~

40 ml (1¼ fl oz) kirsch
20 ml (¾ fl oz) Dubonnet
a twist of lemon peel to garnish

Put the ingredients into a mixing glass,
add plenty of cubed ice and stir gently
until the drink is very cold. Strain into
a chilled glass and add the garnish.

Tastes strong, a little sweet and bitter

Rose
Champagne coupe

~~~~~~~~~~~~~~~~~~~~~~~~~~~~

40 ml (1¼ fl oz) kirsch
2 teaspoons dry vermouth
1 teaspoon raspberry shrub (see page 21)
  or (homemade grenadine, see page 19)
a maraschino cherry to garnish

Put the ingredients into a mixing glass,
add plenty of cubed ice and stir gently
until the drink is very cold. Strain into
a chilled glass and add the garnish.

Tastes strong, a little sweet and aromatic

EPILOGUE

It was the Great Depression, more than any other factor, that ushered in repeal. The US Government simply could not survive without the tax revenue from liquor sales.

When prohibition was repealed, President Roosevelt said, *'What America needs now is a drink.'*

He celebrated with a *Dirty martini,* which from historical accounts he mixed as follows:

a piece of lemon peel
60ml (2 fl oz) dry gin
30ml (1 fl oz) dry vermouth
1 teaspoon olive brine
2 brined olives to garnish

First rub the lemon peel around the rim of a cocktail glass, then discard the peel. Put the rest of ingredients into a shaker, add plenty of cubed ice and shake until the shaker is very frosty. Fine-strain into the prepared glass and add the garnish.

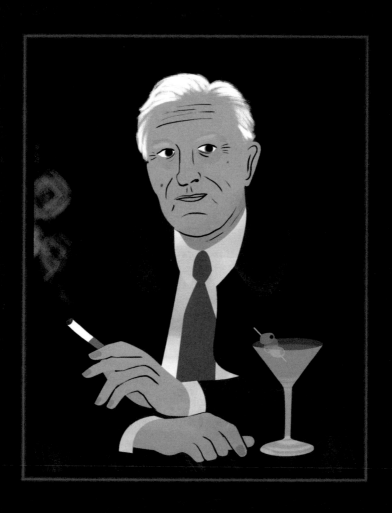

CHEERS!

ACKNOWLEDGEMENTS

I'd like to thank Jakin and Leilani for their perseverance in the face of the weight gain and social discord that necessarily accompany a project like this one; Paul and Lucy for yet another leap; Georgia and Jacqueline for giving real life to this thing; and all of the kindly opportunists that helped me develop the recipes: Zoe, Ali, Pippa, Emely, D.C., Mic, Megan, Captain Dantastic, Seona, Aiden and Alicia – better our collective livers than mine alone.

First published in 2015 by Hardie Grant Books,
an imprint of Hardie Grant Publishing

Hardie Grant Books (Melbourne)
Building 1, 658 Church Street
Richmond, Victoria 3121

Hardie Grant Books (London)
5th & 6th Floors
52–54 Southwark Street
London SE1 1UN

hardiegrantbooks.com

A catalogue record for this
book is available from the
National Library of Australia

SPEAKEASY
ISBN: 978 1 74379 010 6

Publishing Director: Paul McNally
Managing Editor: Lucy Heaver
Editor: Jacqueline Donaldson
Design Manager: Mark Campbell
Designer and Illustrator: Georgia Perry
Production Manager: Todd Rechner

Colour reproduction by Splitting Image Colour Studio

Printed in China by Leo Paper Product. LTD